D0623171

UNIVERSITY OF HOUSTON
MUSIC LIBRARY
106 FINE ARTS
HOUSTON, TEXAS 77204-4893

versity of Houston Libraries

NLS
THEMES OF
SCOTLAND

Ronald
Stevenson

Ronald Stevenson.

NLS THEMES OF SCOTLAND

Ronald Stevenson

A MUSICAL BIOGRAPHY

Malcolm MacDonald

National Library of Scotland
Edinburgh
1989

© National Library of Scotland 1989

All rights reserved. No part of this publication may be reproduced, stored in a retrieval system, or transmitted in any form or by any means, electronic, mechanical, photocopying, recording or otherwise, without the prior permission of the National Library of Scotland.

British Library Cataloguing in Publication Data
MacDonald, Malcolm, *1948-*
    Ronald Stevenson: a musical biography. — (Themes of
    Scotland).
    1. Scottish music. Stevenson, Ronald, 1928-
    I. Title II. National Library of Scotland III. Series
    780'.92'4

    ISBN 0-902220-97-7

Printed on Cream Wove Woodfree Longlife paper.

ACKNOWLEDGEMENTS

All musical examples except Example 2 © copyright by Ronald Stevenson. Examples 1 and 7-11 reproduced by kind permission of Bardic Edition, Aylesbury; Examples 3-6 by kind permission of Roberton Publications, Aylesbury. Examples 1 and 8-11 are reproduced from the composer's manuscript.

Illustrations reproduced by kind permission of Ian Watson (frontispiece); Angus Blackburn (p. viii); Peadar Slattery, FRPS, Dublin (p. 62); and Scotsman Publications Ltd (p. 89).

Cover illustration: Portrait of Ronald Stevenson by Donald Swan, 1989.

ISBN 0-902220-97-7

CONTENTS

For
Derek Watson
and
Jim Reid-Baxter

Civilisation, culture, all the good in the world
Depends ultimately on the existence of a few men of good will.

Hugh MacDiarmid
Lament for the Great Music

Better ae gowden lyric
Than the castle's soaran waa.
Better ae gowden lyric
Than onythin else avaa.

Hugh MacDiarmid
To Circumjack Cencrastus

Stevenson near his Peeblesshire home.

PROLOGUE

NATURE abhors a vacuum, and a straight line. She seems to have created Ronald Stevenson to fill the former, and made it impossible for anyone seeking to understand him to follow the latter. His music is full of independent lines, as befits a master contrapuntist, but their progress is intricately woven, mirroring or responding to one another, criss-crossing and intertwined. His life-work is as complexly patterned and irregular as the knotwork of the Celtic brooches and crosses he so admires: restless, dynamic, doubling back on itself, 'plaited' (to cite a favourite line from Hugh MacDiarmid) 'like the generations of men'. Readers should get their bearings by the simple chronology that follows this work (p.110), but the book itself pursues only a tenuously chronological path. Some account of Stevenson's life is embedded within it; but the main discussion, which is of his work, of necessity ranges ahead of itself, doubles back or diverts into by-ways, to follow the inextricably commingled themes that have shaped his musical character. Great among those themes is that of friendship, actual or spiritual: the rendering of homage is one of his primary creative impulses. So, inevitably, the text introduces many of the composers, writers, and others whose example has variously inspired Stevenson's music. Without them, his own art would be the poorer.

What was the vacuum? I recall an occasion in the early 1960s when television and radio gave some prominence to an address by the then head of BBC Music in Scotland, Watson Forbes, in which he lamented the fact that Scotland's composers had yet to come to terms with her wonderful heritage of folk-music, and called for a 'MacDvořák' to create a national musical language. Even then, with the superiority of my fourteen or so years, I remember thinking this a hopelessly anachronistic requirement, and that in any case we had *had* our 'MacDvořák' — not perhaps in any one commanding figure, but in a long line of decent sub-Romantic composers, from Hamish McCunn to George McIlwham, whose music received a modicum of BBC air-time and manifested a patina of Scots local colouring. What Scotland *really* lacked, I was sure, was a 'MacBartók', who, from the rich heritage of our folk-music (whose existence I largely took on trust), might fashion a truly 20th-century yet fundamentally Scots idiom that could enrich the main stream of European music in our time.

It is comment enough on the state of Scotland's musical self-knowledge that, though already an enthusiast for a broad spectrum of the world's 20th-century music, I had never heard the name of Francis George Scott, who had achieved this forty years before in the field of solo song. And it was to be some years yet before I became aware of Ronald Stevenson, and the fact that he was consciously working towards a 'coalescence' (one of his favourite words) of Celtic folk traditions with the best in European art-music, on a much more epic scale, and seeking even beyond this to create a 'world music' that would unite all the different traditions, East and West, in a grand musical synthesis. This is assuredly not the way in which Mr Forbes envisaged the musical vacuum being filled: but it is how Stevenson has filled it, making of his work a nexus, a place of union ('aonach', in the Gaelic), a region 'whaur extremes meet'. The cornucopic variety and interconnectedness of the many strands of his creative activity make him impossible to define with any discrete, delimiting phrase. He is neither romantic nor modernist, radical, revolutionary nor reactionary, folklorist nor philosopher, realist nor dreamer. He is all of them at once; and he is certainly a melodist, a master of variation, and a prime exponent of the ancient art of transcription.

There is, however, a central aspect to his activities, which will serve at least to orient us as I attempt to provide a mere sketch-map of Ronald Stevenson's life-work. Bayan Northcott of the *Independent* defined it closely in reviewing a performance of Stevenson's most famous work — the *Passacaglia on DSCH* — in 1988:

> The Scottish composer-pianist and Busoni-scholar, Ronald Stevenson, is our most distinguished representative of what might be called the tradition of Philosophical Virtuosity: a tradition in which transcendental pianism is somehow bound up with stylistic eclecticism and the highest ethical ideals, running back via Busoni and Liszt ultimately to late Beethoven.

That is a high lineage indeed: perhaps the very highest. It does not imply that all Stevenson's works are masterpieces (far from it — though at least one can never imagine him writing, as Beethoven did, a *Battle Symphony!*). But in seeking — sometimes at some discomfort to critics and listeners — to reunite ethical idealism with artistic creation, he poses questions that may not be side-stepped. He is the conscience of 20th-century Scottish music, and we ignore the lessons of his work at our peril.

There are many small omissions in this book, and one grievous one. I have had neither the space nor the expert knowledge to include any thorough consideration of Stevenson as a pianist, though his performing activities are second only in importance to his composing. I simply record here my conviction that he can be one of the most exciting performers alive, is a master of all the techniques required by 'transcendental virtuosity', and possesses an intimate understanding of the expressive, singing possibilities of piano tone. A detailed appraisal of his pianism does exist, in an essay by Harold Taylor written for a symposium long ago announced by Toccata Press: to this the reader is directed, if and when it appears. I have also said little about his recital-programming: an art in itself, of which Stevenson is among the boldest and most illuminating exponents.

I could not have undertaken this book without the composer's generous co-operation, in musical materials, hospitality, conversation, and general good humour. The otherwise unidentified quotations from him in the main text are all drawn from tape-recorded discussions between us carried out sporadically between July and December 1988. Marjorie Stevenson also materially contributed to these discussions. I thank, too, Barry Ould of Bravura Edition, Aylesbury, which now handles the bulk of Stevenson's work, for his uncomplaining compliance with my multidudinous requests for scores and tapes; the staff of the Scottish Music Information Centre for the supply of tapes; and that of the Barbican Library for copies of articles.

London
1989

1

YOUTH AND SONG

In the arts, there is only one real teacher: inclination. And he has only one useful assistant: imitation.

Arnold Schoenberg

IN one of the world's premier music dictionaries, *Baker's Dictionary of Music and Musicians,* Ronald Stevenson is described by the distinguished lexicographer Nicolas Slonimsky not as a 'British' but a 'Brythonic' composer and pianist. Perhaps Slonimsky had read, in Hugh MacDiarmid's *Albyn, or Scotland and the Future* (1927), that

> the country between the Humber–Mersey line and the Forth and Clyde line corresponds to the old Brythonic Kingdom. This is our real centre of gravity. Most of our heavy industries are centred there — most of our mineral wealth — and statistics show that an overwhelming percentage of Scottish and English genius alike of all kinds has come from that area.

MacDiarmid's typically trenchant assertion implies that genius lends itself to statistical examination. As Sydney Goodsir Smith would have said, 'mebbe'. But just as Goodsir Smith, a New Zealander who wrote in Scots, is counted one of Scotland's greatest modern poets, so his and MacDiarmid's friend Ronald Stevenson is certainly a Scottish composer — by ancestry, affinity, residence, creative activity, and most of all by the instinctive nature of his musical speech. With a birthplace far to the south of the official Scottish border, though north of the Mersey (he was born in Blackburn, Lancashire, on 6 March 1928), Stevenson is a spiritual citizen of 'the old Brythonic Kingdom', bestriding two cultures, as his music has since sought to bestride many more.

He was the younger of two sons, born to working-class parents of Scottish and Welsh descent. His father was a railway fireman whose forefathers had come to England from Kilmarnock in Ayrshire; his mother worked as a weaver in the Blackburn woollen mills, and *her* mother, who could still speak Welsh, had been a child truck-pusher in the Welsh coalmines back in the 1860s (she is commemorated in the first of her grandson's *Cambrian Cantos* for harp). His maternal grandfather was a bargee on the Leeds–Liverpool canal, and one of Stevenson's earliest memories — after the smell of hops from the Blackburn breweries, and the sound of machinery in the weaving mills — is of the voice of John McCormack, on an early HMV record, wafted across the waters from his grandfather's barge, singing Tom Moore's *Believe me if all those endearing young charms*.

He knew the song already. There were few amenities at home — the only bath was a tin one, in front of the fire — but Stevenson's father had a strong love of music, a pleasant light tenor voice and a rich repertoire of Scottish folksongs, Moore's *Irish Melodies*, and popular favourites from the operas of Balfe and Vincent Wallace. The young Ronald was set to learning the piano from the age of eight, and soon called upon to act as his father's accompanist. It was excellent training, which awoke in him a great love of melody, and a delight (like James Joyce's) in the tenor voice, reflected in a life-long enthusiasm for the recordings of John McCormack, Richard Tauber and Caruso.

Even as a child, he seems to have had a strong streak of romantic idealism. One writes 'even', but of course idealism, imagination, and a sense of wonder are, or should be, natural childhood states: the remarkable thing about Stevenson is how he has managed to preserve those qualities through his adult life. From the first he was strongly attracted to poetry, and while at Darwen Grammar School he would spend hours in the school library copying out personal anthologies of his favourite authors: a significantly Celtic selection — Robert Louis Stevenson, Walter Scott, the half-Irish William Hazlitt, and, above all, Robert Burns.

By contrast, he was at first an unenthusiastic piano pupil — it was only at the age of twelve that he really began to become attracted to music as such. At the time, he was more interested in boxing, and his father bribed him to study by promising a whole boxing outfit if he would learn to play the variations from Flotow's *Martha*. Stevenson senior, like many Scots, 'thrived on thrift', but he was never thrifty with his son, who soon began to manifest unusual musical gifts. Indeed, shortly after the Second World War he bought Ronald a boudoir grand piano, an enormous expense for a railwayman to incur. But by this time the budding pianist and composer (he had started writing music of his own about the age of fourteen, in imitation of the songs his father sang and of the favourite composers he had heard, notably Grieg, Dvořák and Schubert) already had some years' experience playing in concert parties (with his elder brother as a singer and comedian), and as composer and accompanist for the Blackburn Ballet Company; and he had won an open scholarship to the Royal Manchester College of Music at the age of seventeen. Music was clearly going to be his life. But the love of physical exercise made him a keen hill-walker from an early age, taking his volume of Burns with him up on the Darwen moors.

In all likelihood Stevenson's social background, a most unlikely one at the time for anyone studying to be a professional musician, sustained him in the very unconventional interests he pursued at the RMCM. His composition teacher was Richard Hall — some years later to be *éminence grise* for the 'Manchester School' of Alexander Goehr, Harrison Birtwistle and Peter Maxwell Davies, but from whom Stevenson felt he learned virtually nothing; and his principal piano tutor was Iso Elinson, a fine musician who had little gift for teaching, though Stevenson remembers him with great affection, and absorbed (by example rather than precept) the cardinal rule of stroking rather than hitting the keys, thus avoiding extraneous sounds which are amplified by the piano pedals. From Elinson he also absorbed great contrapuntal clarity, making the separate voices 'sing' in the fugues from Bach's *Well-Tempered Clavier*. Stevenson was already, by instinct, a dedicated contrapuntist: for months he would arise at 6.00am and do an hour of pre-breakfast counterpoint exercises from Johann Josef Fux's historic treatise, *Gradus ad Parnassum*.

The cardinal musical experiences of his student days were, however, the discovery of the music of Busoni, a consuming interest right up to the present day; and of the grand virtuoso tradition, stemming from Chopin and Liszt, in which Busoni stood, and whose various examplars in piano-playing and composition — Medtner, Rachmaninoff, d'Albert, Godowsky, Paderewski and Sorabji — has each his honoured niche in Stevenson's personal pantheon. Almost all of these lavishly talented figures were even more desperately unfashionable then than they are now, but Stevenson marvelled at their sovereign mastery of the piano medium, the spontaneity of their invention, and the strongly individualized character of their playing (for instance in Paderewski's own recordings). They set a far more valuable standard for his music and piano technique than any textbook could provide.

Equally important were a number of strong musical friendships, notably with John Ogdon, who wandered into Ronald's life as a nine-year-old boy, drawn fascinated by Stevenson's impromptu score-reading, at the piano in a RMCM rehearsal-room, of Busoni's huge and then almost unknown Piano Concerto: a work Ogdon himself was to perform many times over a decade later, after seeking Stevenson's advice on its interpretation. Other contemporaries included Margaret Holden, later a leading exponent of the Kodály concept of music education (which deeply interests Stevenson), and for whose Blackpool choir he has since written part-songs employing Kodályan principles. Another friend was Irving Wardle, now theatre critic of *The Times*, but then living in Bolton and studying music at Oxford University. Stevenson wrote piano studies for him, and it was Wardle who introduced him to the novels and poetry of James Joyce. With comrades such as Wardle and his fellow-Boltonian Ernest Hall, Stevenson would debate books of strong mutual interest, like Cecil Gray's *Warlock* and Sorabji's *Mi contra Fa*, or read poetry, take long walks, or sleep out on summer nights in the woods. To his love of Burns had been added the searing moral vision of William Blake, and the torrential, world-embracing democratic sincerity of Walt Whitman — two poets whom he counts among the greatest influences on his thought.

Most important of all, Stevenson had fallen in love at first sight with a remote cousin, Marjorie Spedding, who was eventually to become his wife.

As yet, he had little knowledge of politics. He was vaguely aware of socialism: his father read much socialist literature, and as a child

Ronald had heard him deep in conversation with friends at his home, discussing European politics.

I was aware of the serious mien of these plain men. They seemed to know far more than the politicians were saying, about what was going to happen; they knew war was coming. . . . I heard phrases bandied about — the Spanish Civil War, Hitler, Mussolini.

Stevenson aged eleven.

Stevenson was only eleven when war broke out, and the opposition to war as such that gradually took root in him was instinctive but, he thinks, 'vaguely religious' in origin. His feelings were nevertheless strongly anti clerical. He had been baptized in his mother's faith as a Roman Catholic, against his father's wishes; but he gradually saw that no national church had the courage to speak out against war. Rather, all supported it in the interests of the state rather than of the Prince of Peace. Article 37 of the Church of England even legalizes the bearing of arms by Christians in War. His pacifism, which has been a dominating principle of his life, was influenced by his reading of William Blake and Albert Schweitzer, but especially by the realization that, although not old enough to be allowed to vote, and therefore a child in law, he was considered old enough to be trained to kill. In 1947 he graduated from the RMCM with special distinction, and soon faced his call-up for National Service. As a Conscientious Objector, he refused — and was sent to prison instead.

Thus Stevenson experienced his first 'grand tour'. Still a minor in law, he was forced to wear shorts in gaol, even in winter-time. He was moved from prison to prison, often sharing a cell with five or six hardened criminals: from Preston to Liverpool, to the 'Dickensian' Winston Green in Birmingham, and finally to Wormwood Scrubs. ('If the Soviet Union got their hands on this they would have had a wonderful propaganda story — that under the Attlee government, in peacetime, this happened to a young socialist pacifist.') Despite his surroundings, he managed to compose one of his most visionary early piano pieces, the *Chorale Prelude for Jean Sibelius*, in Wormwood Scrubs. He read the Bible straight through twice, and Albert Schweitzer's *Bach* three times — a telling index of his opinion of their relative merits.

Among British composers he knew of, Michael Tippett had received like treatment — but that was in wartime, and Tippett was older, and had not been imprisoned for so long. Stevenson wrote to Tippett, who recommended an appeal to the Appellate Tribunal to be allowed to take the 'Agricultural Condition' of directed labour on the land. As a result, he was sent to Freighting Hall, Essex, near Colchester, a farm for conscientious objectors run by the poet J.H. Watson — a friend of Middleton Murry and the Blake expert Max Plowman, and a passionate disciple of D.H. Lawrence. (Stevenson set one of Watson's poems as a carol for chorus.) Stevenson did not work out the whole of his sentence in these surroundings, however, but ended up ditching and draining in the company of Irish navvies, who must have found his vegetarianism even odder than his compulsion to write music. It was in the intervals between work, in the evenings, or sheltering from rain in cowsheds that he completed a central and highly personal work of this youthful period — settings for voice and piano of the whole of William Blake's *Songs of Innocence*.

Stevenson's earliest surviving compositions are concentrated in the fields of song and of piano music — an impression we would have to modify were his pieces for Blackburn Ballet Company still extant; even in their absence, they should remind us that he was equally mindful of the claims of the Dance. (He remembers with affection a Dvořákian waltz for orchestra, and a ballet on *Peter and the Wolf* written in total ignorance of Prokofiev.) From the beginning, there was a pull towards Scotland: his first songs were settings of poems such as Byron's *So we'll go no more a-roving* (derived from an old Aberdeenshire ballad) and Walter Scott's *Violets*, and they grew directly out of the experience of accompanying his father's singing of Tom Moore's *Irish Melodies* and Scots folksongs — music fashionable in the London salons of the 1820s which, in the course of the succeeding century, had percolated through to the working-class consciousness. With the voracious instinct of the true creator, the fourteen-year-old Stevenson began by imitating whatever lay closest to hand, and the strong lyrical impulse in these direct, frankly melodic songs gives them a musical interest above ordinary juvenilia. Speaking forty-five years later of *Violets*, for instance, the composer could dissect its likely origins and its latent possibilities.

> I can trace . . . the *Lyric Pieces* of Grieg, I can trace Paderewski's piano playing, even one piece of Paderewski's — *Chant du voyageur* — and my absorption of pentatony and the Scots snap, the idioms of Scottish folk-music. All intuitive. And yet there's another thing in that piece which is very conscious, and that is the early realization (I suppose I thought of line-drawing) that melody is

the profile of music, and the bass completes its human face.... I realized it was necessary to write a tune and to have a good bass line. And how I did that was very often to write a bass line which was an inversion of the melody, a kind of mirror inversion; or I would do it crossing hands pianistically, and imagine that I was playing a tune in the treble but actually playing it in the bass, beneath the chords, and taking account of how it related to the melody, and [*Violets*] is a good example of it.

The awareness, there described, of the *melodic* relation of a bass line to a tune bespeaks the instincts of the born contrapuntist. That aspect is naturally far more prominent in the substantial number of instrumental works Stevenson completed in the second half of the 1940s — such as the first three Piano Sonatinas, the *18 Variations on a Bach Chorale*, and the Violin Sonata. Productions of his student days in Manchester and of the difficult following years, they reflect an ever-widening knowledge of contemporary music and of pianistic tradition, a rapidly-developing compositional skill, a gift for trenchant statement, and no small ambition.

The Piano Sonatinas, for instance, are neither 'simple' nor 'little' sonatas, but quite taxing, structurally expansive works, progressively more assured in technique and exploratory in attitude to form. No. 1 (1945) already shows, for a student piece, a surprisingly sure sense of linear direction in its part-writing, a positive delight in pungent tonal clashes. No. 2 (1947) begins to deviate from expected patterns, with its two-movement form of a florid neo-Baroque Adagietto followed by a virtuosic and cheerfully tuneful finale; while No. 3 (1948), the biggest of them, begins with an almost Mahlerian funeral march — an early 'glimpse of a war-vision' — only to banish it with a glittering scherzo and a highly rhythmic finale of bubbling, eldritch humour. Though not so designated, the suite of *Nativity Pieces* (1949) appears to develop directly out of the concerns of the Sonatinas, its three large movements beginning with a Children's March and including a gorgeously evocative Arabesque-Waltz. In Stevensonian terms, it recalls both Liszt's *Christmas-Tree Suite* and Busoni's *Nuit de Nöel*.

Alongside this prodigious output of instrumental music, his interest in song was unabated, and distinguished at this period by concentration on a single poet: William Blake. The settings of Blake's *Songs of Innocence*, already mentioned, are directly lyrical and deeply felt — a document of considerable human interest, whose evocations of the purity and wonder of childhood must have made an ironic contrast to the harshness of the surroundings in which they were composed. The nineteen songs were written for Stevenson himself to sing (or croak, as he would have it), with little thought to immediate practicalities of performance; but they end with a chorale for mixed voices, *On Another's Sorrow*, which surely enshrines the kernel of his personal beliefs at this time.

Can I see another's woe,
And not be in sorrow too?

In stunning contrast to the lyricism of these settings stands *War* (1947), subtitled 'a dramatic piece': a gripping vocal scena, the most trenchant and explosive musical manifestation of Stevenson's pacifism (and indeed his anti-clericalism). It sets a little-known Blake text, the Prologue to an intended drama, *Edward the Fourth* — a vision of the horrors of war. A baritone part of great range and declamatory force combines with a keyboard accompaniment of extreme virtuosity to produce an excoriating denunciation of human folly, conjuring up a tumultuous succession of musical images to match Blake's evocation of the catastrophe,

When Sin claps his broad wings over the battle,
And sails rejoicing in the flood of Death.

The end of the piece is however a shocked, quiet adagio: grim, solemn chords, *senza espressione*, accompany the baritone's plea to God not to believe that the destruction is merely the doing of the Kings and princes:

Hear it not, Heaven, thy Ministers have done it!

War may indeed be the most personal and cogent achievement among all Stevenson's early music. As a cry from the heart whose expressive force is perfectly matched by the concentration of its technique, it remains as impressive — and as resonant — today as when he wrote it, and unlike any other English song one can think of.

Example 1

Indeed, all these pieces, vocal and instrumental, seem to relate remarkably little to the commonly-performed British music of the time – to Walton, Vaughan Williams, Britten, or Rawsthorne. One can trace in them the emergence of a characteristic harmonic idiom contrasting highly chromatic writing, often expressed in tight-knit semitonal figures, with a luminous diatonicism based upon primal triads. The range of the harmonic language and the steely polyphonic skill resembles that of comparably isolated composers such as Alan Bush and Bernard Stevens – both of whom Stevenson would later befriend, but of whom at this time he knew almost nothing. The works' predominant stance is Eurocentric, and, moreover, concentrated upon aspects of European tradition which were then deeply unfashionable in Britain. An early Minuet for oboe and piano

13

Stevenson aged nineteen.

(1947), subtitled *Hommage to Hindemith*, might seem to indicate a model for Stevenson's contrapuntal methods; but it little resembles Hindemith's own style, and its large form with three trios, the second and third varying the first and progessively tilting the melody towards a shape that encompasses all twelve notes, hints at rather different exemplars.

Such hints become more explicit in perhaps the most ambitious of all these early works, the Sonata for Violin and Piano (1947–48), originally entitled *Sonatina Concertante*. A real duo-sonata, demanding quite as much virtuosity from the pianist as from the violinist, this is cast in a large, complex single movement with several contrasting subdivisions, including a theme with variations, a passacaglia (variations on an unchanging ground bass), and fughetta. Moreover, each of these mini-movements is itself based on successive variations of the idea of the opening *Moderato maestoso*, making the whole work a species of variation-form, and one of Stevenson's first ambitious attempts to oppose the unitary and elaborative processes of variations to the binary, competitive methods of sonata-form. It is difficult to find a model for this profoundly un-classical treatment of form, unless it be the Second Violin Sonata of Busoni. But the work's continual exploration of small groups of notes, expressed as obsessive chromatic motifs, points forward to the motivic preoccupations – unlocking the potential latent in just a few tones – that would eventually give birth to the *Passacaglia on DSCH*. As in the oboe Minuet, continuous development leads in the Sonata's fughetta-finale to the revelation that the work has been based on a 12-note row. Even this early, Stevenson was manifesting a keen (if sometimes wary) interest in the possibilities of Arnold Schoenberg's 12-note method, at least for the purposes of thematic unification, and in a broadly tonal context.

A very different specimen of his early contrapuntal mastery is the *Fugue on a Fragment of Chopin*, written in 1949 to commemorate the centenary of Chopin's death. One thinks of Busoni's early *Variations and Fugue on Chopin's C-minor Prelude*, but Stevenson's work is much the tauter. He is, however, just as bold in taking a very well-known Chopin theme (in this case from the F minor Ballade) and subjecting it to a remarkable range of polyphonic devices to create a personal homage to a pianistic master. At the piece's still centre there is an almost dream-like quotation, 'Aus der Ferne' (from afar), of a canonic passage in Chopin's own work, which Stevenson opens out into multi-layered sonorities marked *velato* (veiled); and, abandoning the strictness of fugue at the end, there is a scherzo-finale in the manner of a tarantella, such as Busoni substituted for his fugue when he re-wrote his Chopin-Variations towards the end of his life.

Already, therefore, 'homages' abound in Stevenson's music: overt ones to Chopin and Hindemith (and to Sibelius), more covert ones to Busoni and even Schoenberg. If it was his instinct to use whatever came to hand, it was also his instinct to salute figures he admired, to build bridges, to celebrate others' achievements. In his comparative intellectual isolation, it was vital to people his music with friends.

Having worked out the term of his sentence, Stevenson returned to Blackburn, and the beginning of a long period without work of any kind (though illuminated by the visit to Gerda Busoni described in a later chapter). He applied for jobs teaching music in schools — a post for which he was if anything over-qualified in purely musical terms, though not, of course, in teaching experience; but the requirement, on all application forms, to give the dates of the applicant's National Service, marked him out at once as a Conscientious Objector, and out of more than 30 applications he was only twice so much as called for an interview.

The second of these was for a music specialist at Boldon Colliery School in County Durham, equidistant between Newcastle-upon-Tyne and Sunderland. Much to his surprise, Stevenson got the job — and it was suggested to him afterwards that in that part of the world, the strongly socialist North-East of England, his pacifism had counted in his favour. It was really only now, under the impact of these post-RMCM experiences, that his political beliefs began to crystallize. He was a year and a half in Boldon Colliery, teaching both boys and girls; for someone new to teaching it must have been a kind of baptism of fire, for he was never a natural disciplinarian. But he made some good friends and gained valuable experience in practical music-making, taking (since it was a mining district) a boys' brass band after school hours, for which he made many arrangements of staple favourites such as Sousa marches.

Stevenson was fascinated by the folk-music that he heard in the area (a continuing fascination, reflected years later in a piano version of the folksong *The Water of Tyne*); but it reminded him strongly of the Scots folksongs he already knew, and kept awake his childhood longing for Scotland.

His cousin Marjorie, who had herself hoped to pursue a musical career, had meanwhile suffered the hard fortune of being disowned by her parents for associating with Ronald. She went to Dartington Hall, the famous arts community in Devon, to work as a domestic servant to the Elmhurst family: there she was befriended by Imogen Holst, who, having heard her play, arranged for her to receive a scholarship to the Music School in 1948-49. But Marjorie was unhappy in Dartington, and eventually left, afterwards taking up factory work. In April 1951 she went to Edinburgh, finding work in factories making electrical components. Ronald resolved to join her, and in the summer of 1952 he 'took the plunge': he left Boldon and set off, with no immediate job prospects, for his ancestral Scotland.

Ferruccio Busoni.

2

MAGISTRI IN ABSENTIA

Who can think wise or stupid things at all
That were not thought already in the Past?

Goethe
Faust

IN the old Royal Manchester College of Music was an anteroom, a
'torture-chamber', where students waited in fear and trembling
before going on to play in recitals. Stevenson found 'an ever-
present injunction to industry' in a drawing which hung there. It was
by Emil Fuchs, and depicted the composer-pianist Busoni as a young
man (Busoni often played in Manchester before his death in 1924).
Stevenson was already attracted by the magnificent music of the
name: Ferruccio Dante Michelangelo Benvenuto Busoni. Then, in
1946, when he was eighteen, he discovered the vocal score of Busoni's
last work, the magico-mystical opera *Doktor Faust*, in the Henry
Watson Music Library. Travelling back to Blackburn by rail, through a
night of Dickensian fog and snow, in the 'voluptuous silence' of an
overheated L.M.S. compartment, he opened the score — and
experienced an immediate, Joycean epiphany: the realization of an
overwhelming affinity with the creator of this questing and visionary
music, an affinity that he admits has exceeded any other in his life.

He felt he had to discover everything about Busoni: and it was badly
in need of discovery. He devoured all the scores in the available
libraries, and (long before photocopying) began transcribing vast
amounts of Busoni's music: the whole of *Faust*, portions of *Arlecchino*,
the *Turandot Suite*, the *Klavierübung*, the Bach-Busoni Chorale
Preludes, and many more. Before long he had conceived the project of
a book about this fascinating and little-understood figure, and had
begun the researches that would occupy him intensively for two
decades, and have continued to the present day.

Stevenson's discovery of Busoni radically affected his attitude to the
craft of composition, and to the career of composer. Busoni was then

(and perhaps is still) best remembered mainly as a piano virtuoso and transcriber, the lesser half of the equation 'Bach-Busoni'. Yet he was one of the supreme all-round musicians of his age. The Busoni whom Stevenson discovered represented many vital ideas.

He was a moral idealist who had expounded the principles of Marxism to German workers on street-corners in Leipzig, and whose pacifism led him to voluntary exile in Switzerland during the First World War.

He was a master contrapuntist, inspired orchestrator, gifted writer, and savant of all the techniques of variation, who stood in a close and yet critical relationship to tradition, worked in the widest possible range of forms, and rejected as juvenile illusion the pursuit of 'originality' *per se*.

He was a passionate advocate of 'the One-ness of Music', a principle of creative eclecticism through which every musical experience became grist to the composer's mill, whether Schoenbergian 'atonality' or the traditional songs of the North American Indians (which formed the basis for three of his works). He continually synthesized disparate elements to create new entities, yet scorned to formulate any closed system of composition. A bi-cultural composer, Tuscan-born and German-trained, he united an Italianate love of song with Bachian polyphonic discipline, the *gaiezza latina* of the Commedia dell'Arte (in his comic opera *Arlecchino*) with the Gothic ethos and philosophical profundity of occult and mystical drama (in his *Faust*).

He was a dedicated transcriber of other composers' works (Bach most famously, but also Schoenberg, Mozart, Liszt, Paganini, and many more), who held that 'it was possible for the piano to take possession of the entire literature of music'.

He was a virtuoso pianist of the first rank who had developed the twin Lisztian traditions of extrovert bravura and restless spiritual exploration; whose knowledge of the instrument's possibilities, enshrined in his monumental *Klavierübung*, his many transcriptions, and his analytical editions of Bach, furnished virtually a complete piano method.

He was an inspiring teacher whose pupils, for piano or for

composition, had included Egon Petri, Percy Grainger, Bernard Van Dieren, and Kurt Weill, while such 20th-century pioneers as Edgard Varèse and Alois Hába were among his protégés.

He was a champion and visionary prophet of new music, who personally financed and conducted concerts of his contemporaries, and whose seminal *Sketch for a New Aesthetic of Music* (1907) adumbrated new modal systems and divisions of the octave smaller than a semitone.

And he was the pioneer of 'Junge Klassizität' (not Neo-Classicism but 'Youthful Classicality') — an antidote to post-Wagnerian Teutonic heaviness, a Mozartian ideal of utter clarity and mastery of technique, selecting from the best of previous developments and embodying them in new and beautiful shapes — which could 'express in well-defined form something of the infinity which surrounds human life'.

Stevenson's detailed study of the life-work of this many-faceted genius was, in effect, a musical self-education more profound and far-reaching than any education his formal teachers could provide. In 1950, unemployed and apparently unemployable, he sold most of his books and gramophone records, and gave a special piano recital, to raise the money to visit Gerda Busoni, the composer's Swedish widow, now blind and living in her native Stockholm. Their meeting initiated a friendship and correspondence that lasted the rest of Gerda's life. It was the first of many journeys — to Germany, Italy, and Switzerland — and the start of a world-wide network of correspondence undertaken in pursuit of Busoni studies. Stevenson's book on the composer was largely written in the 1950s and 1960s, and remains his literary *magnum opus*, although even now it has not been published — its size and scope have so far militated against the commercial 'practicalities' of publishing. Nevertheless, he quickly gained a reputation as one of the leading Busoni authorities in the English-speaking world. He has published many articles on the composer, given broadcast talks and public lecture-recitals of his music, devised and presented a television documentary, and introduced entire series of radio programmes on his life and work.

Busoni's influence was early made manifest in his own music, as noted in the previous chapter. Stevenson's earliest works for full orchestra were a *Berceuse symphonique* (1951), clearly imbued with elements of Busoni's orchestral masterpieces, *Berceuse élégiaque* and *Nocturne symphonique*, and a set of *Waltzes* (1952) that pays homage to Busoni's late and brilliant dance-piece, the *Tanzwalzer*. Even earlier than these was a solo-piano *Fantasy on 'Doktor Faust'* (1949), which he played to Gerda Busoni in Stockholm — a brilliantly eventful and glitteringly virtuosic study on themes from Busoni's opera, recreating the Lisztian tradition of operatic fantasy, just as Busoni had done in his *Kammerfantasie on Bizet's 'Carmen'*. The Faustian obsession led Stevenson on to compose a *Fugue on 'Clavis Astartis Magica'* (1950) — the theme of the magic book, 'The Key to Stellar Magic', given to Faust by three ghostly students in the opera's opening scene.

Example 2

BUSONI

STEVENSON

Whereas the *Faust Fantasy* is by turns anguished, lyrical and infused with Mephistophelean energy, the 'Clavis' Fugue is aloof, severe — the first example in Stevenson's music of a withdrawn, occult, hermetic vein that probes spiritual mysteries through the manipulation of notes as symbols of an unrevealed truth. The nine successive pitches of the theme become the tonalities of its later entries, determining the fugue's structure. Stevenson, a dedicated — indeed compulsive — practitioner of the form, still thinks this poised yet restlessly meditative music the finest fugue he has ever written.

It was John Ogdon who, in 1959, suggested that these *Faust* piano pieces should be combined with a prelude developing the same material, to produce a large-scale triptych. The result was the *Prelude, Fugue and Fantasy on Busoni's 'Faust'*, the synoptic piano work which sums up much of Stevenson's early compositional development, and which, eventually published in the 'Virtuoso' Modern Piano Series edited by Ogdon, has become one of his best-known achievements. Nor did its evolution end there: in 1960 Stevenson further expanded and rewrote it for piano and orchestra as his Piano Concerto No. 1, *A Faust Triptych*. He has also transcribed several of Busoni's original works for different media, among then the *Quartettino* (1965), a transcription for string quartet of a favourite piano work, Busoni's *Sonatina ad usum infantis*.

In his explorations of Busoni, Stevenson encountered or found himself re-evaluating other figures who were to assume great importance for him. An obvious one was the Finnish master Jean Sibelius, who had been a close friend of Busoni and corresponded with Stevenson until his death in 1957. Far less well known was Bernhard Ziehn (1845-1912), a German musicologist who settled in Chicago. He evolved a contrapuntal method based on symmetrical inversion of intervals, providing Busoni with the impetus for his polyphonic masterpiece *Fantasia contrappuntistica* (based on the unfinished fugue from Bach's *Art of Fugue*), and significantly affecting his later music. Stevenson, too, studied and used Ziehn's technique, and eventually edited the first modern publication (Kahn & Averill, 1976) of his seminal textbook, *Canonical Studies*, writing an explanatory preface to it.

Another important figure was the Dutch-born but British-domiciled composer Bernard Van Dieren (1887-1936), a friend of Busoni and Schoenberg, and a man of wide general culture, who showed great physical courage in the face of a crippling illness. A friend of Arnold Bennett and the Sitwell brothers, he wrote a book on the sculpture of Jacob Epstein, as well as one of the classics of British musical polemic, the essay-collection *Down Among the Dead Men*. He had been highly valued by Peter Warlock and Cecil Gray, although his compositions had met with very little public acceptance. Stevenson was fascinated by Van Dieren's hard-won serenity, the freedom and flexibility of his polyphonic writing, his mastery of cadence, and his rich harmony which could nonetheless accommodate Hebridean pentatony (for Van Dieren made a setting of the *Eriskay Love-Lilt*). In 1951, Stevenson transcribed Van Dieren's song *Weep you no more, Sad Fountains*, both as a piano piece and as 'a Consolation for small orchestra' — the first of several transcriptions and editions of his music.

Such preoccupations gave rise to one of Stevenson's most private works, a collection of sixteen piano pieces he wrote between 1956 and 1959 and entitled *A 20th-Century Music Diary*. This is no diary of random jottings or anecdotes, however, but a purposeful series of brief studies in the creative problems and possibilities confronting one highly individual musical mind. The opening 'Preludio al corale' is a Ziehn-like study in the enharmonic unity of triadic and quartal harmony; the ensuing pieces explore canonic techniques, strict counterpoint, symmetrical inversion, Busonian modal scales, polytonality, and chromaticism taken to the brink of atonality, often on motifs whose symbolic overtones conjure up tutelary spirits from the past. Piece No. 9 is a canon 'In Memoriam Bernard van Dieren'. No. 10 takes the name B–A–C–H and subjects it to a fantastic Lisztian 'nocturnal cavalcade', making exhaustive, Schoenbergian use of all twenty-four of the motif's possible permutations. Nos. 11 and 12 are miniature sets of seven variations each, the former on a 12-note row derived from the Statue Scene in Mozart's *Don Giovanni*, the latter on the angular, tritonal theme of Mephistopheles from Berlioz's *Damnation of Faust*. No. 13 is a fugal invention on a theme, from

Busoni's opera *Arlecchino*, that spells out four successive triads a semitone apart and so encompasses all twelve notes; No. 14 is a fugal exposition on the 12-note 'Faust' theme from Liszt's *Faust-Symphonie*. These tiny, intense studies were highly important for Stevenson in clarifying his compositional technique (and peopling his compositional universe); and the *20th-Century Music Diary* contained the seeds of several subsequent works — among them the *Four Meditations* for string quartet (1964), and the elusive, yet on close acquaintance deeply moving, *Prelude and Fugue on a 12-note theme from Liszt's Faust-Symphonie* (1961–62), a substantial organ composition that takes its cue from No. 14 of the *Diary* to produce perhaps the most impressively 'hermetic' of all Stevenson's creations.

His Busoni researches led him also to a very different figure — the Australian composer and pianist Percy Grainger, who had studied with Busoni and was still active and living in the USA. A lively correspondence ensued. In Stevenson's own estimation, Grainger 'provided a healthy antidote' to his Busoni mania:

> Although he [Grainger] admired Busoni as a pianist and as a teacher, he had many reservations about him as a composer. I remember that he took particular exception to Busoni's concept of music itself as an architectonic structure. Grainger, having come from the wide open spaces of Australia, felt that the nature of music was not like an architectural edifice, but rather like a ribbon rolled along the floor that gradually describes a single line.[1]

If Busoni was the primary shaping force on Stevenson's music, Grainger was the second, and perhaps the more dearly loved of the two. As a teenager, Stevenson had taken a rather lofty attitude to Grainger's well-known 'titbits', such as *Shepherd's Hey* and *Handel in the Strand*. Personal contact forced him to reassess music and man. Grainger's utter lack of pomposity; his tumultuous, unfettered pianism; his desire to rid music of jargon and break the artistic

---

1. 'Composer's Anthology 3. Ronald Stevenson' — text of a lecture given on 6 March 1969 at the British Institute of Recorded Sound and reprinted in the BIRS journal *Recorded Sound* No. 42-43 (1971) p.750. Hereafter cited as 'Composer's Anthology'.

Percy Grainger.

dominance of middle-European tradition; his passion for the mountain regions of the Scandinavian North and the Celtic North-West, among them the 'soul-shaking hillscapes of Western Argyllshire'; his personal collecting of folksongs 'in the field' from those areas and from the Rocky Mountains, Lincolnshire, Polynesia and China, and his robustly unsentimental 'dishing-up' of them as incisively characterized miniature compositions; his love of jazz, bagpipe music, wind-band and choral composition; his longing for a 'free' music of aboriginal immediacy, and his researches into electronic techniques to achieve this; his passion for Icelandic Saga, for Whitman and for Kipling, especially *The Jungle Book* (which led Stevenson to dub him 'Music's Mowgli'); his humour, his vege-tarianism and love of physical exercise — all these provided a drastic counterpoise to the mystical, involved, hyper-cultured imaginative world of Busoni. Grainger's entire *attitude* was different, and came to Stevenson as a breath of fresh air. In seeking to synthesize what he learned from these two utterly contrasting figures, he would enlarge his own work and give it a new sense of direction.

Stevenson's epistolary friendship with Grainger lasted until Grainger's death in 1961, and continued with his widow Ella into the 1970s. Grainger's music has since experienced a revival of popularity, but in the 1950s and early 1960s it had long gone out of fashion, and Stevenson was therefore one of the pioneers of its rediscovery. Thus was engendered a further series of musical tributes — two of Stevenson's most ambitious and effective virtuoso piano trans-criptions are of major Grainger orchestral scores: the seldom-heard *Hill-Song No. 1* (lovingly and elaborately arranged by Stevenson in 1960, much to Grainger's delight, and premièred by John Ogdon at the 1966 Aldeburgh Festival), and the passacaglia *Green Bushes* (1963). Also in 1960 he composed his own orchestral *Jamboree for Grainger*, a cheerful pot-pourri on well-loved Grainger themes, which in the late 1980s became the starting-point for metamorphosis into a virtuosic and many-faceted concertante work for piano, wind band and percussion, entitled *Corroborree for Grainger*. He has subsequently edited various Grainger works, notably his treatments of Scottish folksongs and specially simplified editions for young players.

Stevenson's setting of 'The Lea', by William Soutar.

A further long-distance friendship of great significance for Stevenson was with the actor, theatre-designer, producer of drama and opera, writer, editor, wood-engraver, etcher, lithographer and occasional composer, Edward Gordon Craig (1872-1966), the son of Ellen Terry and pupil of Henry Irving. Stevenson approached him in 1953 on the subject of puppet-theatre, a concept that had fascinated Busoni, and on whose possibilities Craig was probably the foremost philosopher — his seminal essay *The Actor and the Über-Marionette* had been written in the same year as Busoni's *New Aesthetic*. But their correspondence continued for thirteen years, on a host of topics of mutual interest (Craig had actually heard Liszt play in London, while his brilliantly simple and revolutionary ideas on the use of lighting to create dramatic scenic effects fascinated Stevenson), and was a very significant life-line for the young composer through his first, difficult years in Scotland. To the end, into his nineties, Craig was an incomparable and inspiring correspondent, full of life and quenchless enthusiasm.[2] Stevenson remembers his friendship and support with particular gratitude, and counts him one of the main influences on his life.

2. Since one of the many loves of Craig's life had been the great dancer Isadora Duncan, it is interesting to note that in the early 1950s Stevenson sketched (but has not completed) an orchestral *Suite for Isadora Duncan.*

3

'LANG HAE WE PAIRTED BEEN'

O Scotland is
THE barren fig

Hugh MacDiarmid
A Drunk Man Looks at the Thistle

STEVENSON arrived in Edinburgh — where Marjorie had been working since April 1951 — without job prospects or any clear idea of the musical possibilities. After spending 'the statutory fortnight at the Y.M.C.A.' he married Marjorie at Church Hill registry office, and secured a temporary teaching job at Norton Park school. This was the beginning of an eleven-year period, until 1963, during which he taught music in a variety of Edinburgh schools, among them Carrickvale, Niddrie Marischal and finally Broughton High School; he also did some private teaching of piano and composition, and took evening classes as a lecturer for the Workers' Educational Association. The routine was broken by a number of recital tours, as a pianist, to various parts of the UK; and (in 1955) by a six-month sojourn in Rome, researching for his Busoni book on an Italian Government Scholarship, and studying orchestration with Guido Guerrini — himself a biographer and pupil of Busoni — at the Conservatorio di Santa Cecilia. One fruit of this period was the major article 'Busoni: the Legend of a Prodigal', which Stevenson published in 1956 in William Glock's prestigious modern-music magazine *The Score*. Another was friendship with the young Rumanian composer Roman Vlad and the older Italian master Ildebrando Pizzetti, from Parma. Stevenson has since composed two sets of variations on a theme from Pizzetti's *La Pisanella*, the first for piano and the later (dedicated to Josef Szigeti) for unaccompanied violin. On his return from Italy he began to lecture and perform more widely: notably at Dartington Hall Summer School in 1956, at the First International Busoni Festival in Empoli, Tuscany, in 1958, and in 1962 as a lecturer in the

Department of Extra-Mural Studies of Edinburgh University.

Initially the Stevensons lived in Edinburgh, where their son Gordon (named for Edward Gordon Craig) was born in 1953. While Ronald was researching in Rome, Marjorie worked as a House-Mother for Garvald House, the Rudolf Steiner school for mentally handicapped children in Dolphinton, Peeblesshire; on his return they lived for a while in a cottage in the school courtyard, before moving in 1956 to the nearby village of West Linton. Stevenson has kept up a close connexion with Garvald, often arranging music for the annual Christmas concert for the children; and in 1965 he composed the school song, *One and All*, to his own translation of Christian Morgenstern's poem *Eins und Alles*, for unison children's voices, recorder, violin, cello and guitar.

At West Linton, in the second of the three houses they occupied there during 1956, the Stevensons' first daughter was born – delivered by the composer himself in the absence of a midwife, and named Gerda after Gerda Busoni; their second daughter, Ella Savourna (named for Ella Grainger), followed in 1961. The cottage in which they finally took up residence, Townfoot House, had once been the home of the fiddler-composer Archibald Bain, one of the two reputed 'composers' (more likely arrangers – the tune itself is probably of Gaelic origin) of the well-known reel *The High Road to Linton*. Bain had filled the rooms with manuscript music, most of it sold and dispersed after his death. Stevenson, who has made versions of the reel for piano and for fiddle and clarsach, proceeded to fill them anew.

Although as a school-teacher he made some good and close friends, especially at Broughton, Stevenson freely admits that they were not particularly happy years. He was an instinctively unconventional figure, looking more the part of a turn-of-the-century virtuoso with his Paderewskian moustache and broad-brimmed black sombrero (although his pupils, with a different range of reference, nicknamed him 'Buffalo Bill'). He felt 'a square peg in a round hole'; nor did he consider himself a particularly good teacher of music. (However, his enthusiasm and wide-ranging interests certainly communicated themselves to some of his pupils and members of his W.E.A. classes.) Moreover, his contacts with Edinburgh musicians were at first quite limited, and although he early met the composers Robert Crawford and Hans Gál, and was able to have some of his works performed under the aegis of Edinburgh University Music Society, the 1950s hardly constituted a period of glittering public achievement for the young composer-pianist.

> Hugh MacDiarmid once said, 'Scotland is the most backward country in Europe, aesthetically speaking'. From my experience of living there, I am convinced that it is true. There is no feigned sophistication there, but rather a crude, healthy philistinism that hits you in the face. That is a challenge for me: at least it is honest.[1]

Outside the Edinburgh Festival, and in contrast to the situation today, there seemed to be little musical activity, and especially few opportunities for Scottish composers (or composers with decisively Scottish interests). As a centre for art-music, as distinct from her more vigorous and resilient folk traditions, Scotland had suffered a long decline since the Renaissance, when the masses and motets of the Canon of Scone, Robert Carver (1487-1566), attained a peak of polyphonic genius fully comparable with the greatest of his European contemporaries. While 18th-century Edinburgh attracted important Continental musicians and had boasted such characterful composers as Sir John Clerk of Penicuik (a pupil of Corelli), the sonata-composer and fiddler William McGibbon, and the symphonist Thomas Erskine, 6th Earl of Kelly — all of them familiar with and influenced by folk-instrumental traditions — by the mid-19th century Scotland was relegated to a musical backwater, its composers in the shadow of Victorian England's German-derived musical orthodoxy.

The later 19th-century stirrings of musical nationalism, so strongly represented in Bohemia by Smetana and Dvořák, in Russia by Tchaikovsky and 'the Five', in Scandinavia by Grieg and later Sibelius, found a faint echo in the work of such (London-trained) Scots as Hamish McCunn and Learmont Drysdale. But the genuine re-engagement with the resources of various countries' folk-music, pioneered by the Romantic Nationalists of Europe and then taken up more radically in a search for genuinely new and distinctive means

---

1. Composer's Anthology, p.752.

of musical expression (by Bartók and Kodály in Hungary, or Szymanowski in Poland, for example) seemed largely to have passed Scotland by. Native composers of a genuinely exploratory outlook were forced either to pursue their careers elsewhere, or were consigned to obscurity.[2] Those who had attained some national prominence through the BBC, such as Cedric Thorpe Davie and Ian Whyte, were not insignificant musicians, but on any European scale their achievement was of strictly limited scope.

In this unpromising cultural landscape, a composer of Stevenson's passionate intensity and breadth of enthusiasm could hardly be assured of an instant welcome, or even understanding. In fact, the vital musical experiences of his early years in Scotland did not involve the existing art-music establishment, such as that was, but haphazard yet arresting encounters with aspects of Celtic music — the strong, rich folk-tradition which impressed him far more than the efforts of any contemporary Scots 'classical' composer of his acquaintance. One such revelation was hearing, over the radio in 1956, the song 'From an Old Pibroch', performed by the great Gaelic singer James Campbell of Kintail — a supremely haunting tune of which Stevenson was subsequently to make several settings. But his first comprehensive attunement to the world of Gaelic song occurred when he was thirty, in 1958, on the island of Islay, while taking part in a Scottish Arts Council tour of Argyll and the Inner Hebrides.

I was solo pianist and accompanist. Our troupe also included a violinist, an 'elocutionist' (a surviving phenomenon of Edwardian culture) and a singer, Evelyn Campbell from Lewis. She sang a mixed repertoire of accompanied songs and unaccompanied Gaelic folk songs. While she sang in Gaelic, I eavesdropped in the wings. The audience very softly joined in the

---

2. An example of the latter was the indubitably gifted Aberdeenshire composer Ronald Center (1913-73), whose dissonant, post-Bartókian style found little favour in the 1940s and who eked out his existence as a schoolmaster and private teacher in Huntly. Stevenson, who greatly esteems Center's music, knew little of it until after Center's death; he has since given several posthumous premières of Center's works, and recorded his Piano Sonata for Altarus Records.

choruses ... I could see they also gently swayed as they sang; and I could hear them keeping time with the music by quietly tapping their feet to emphasize the main rhythmic beats. The general mood of the music was characterized by a low, melodious moan. Few of the songs were humorous or spirited. I later realized that this ratio of much sweet melancholy, some stoicism and a little spirited humour was basic to ... the great body of Gaelic poetry.[3]

Not long afterwards, in the Abbotsford pub in Edinburgh, Stevenson made the acquaintance of Hector MacIver (1910-66), the Lewis-born writer, broadcaster and schoolmaster, an unforgettable storyteller ('seanachaidh', in Gaelic) who had himself collected folksongs in the Isles. There in the pub MacIver sang

strangely serene psalm tunes in the Gaelic, with no less than ten, and sometimes more than a dozen, notes to each syllable. Such long-linked melismas I had never heard in any other vocal music. They suggested a vocal 'transcription' of highly ornamented bagpipe music. They also suggested those curious involuted knot-designs of Celtic carvings, brooches and crosses.[4]

Stevenson counted this as his initiation into the rhythmic intricacy of Gaelic music. Meanwhile, chance had given him access to a large body of Irish song. The Deputy Head at Broughton during Stevenson's time there was the novelist and ex-sailor John Sinclair: a passionate enthusiast of Irish folksong, especially songs in Irish Gaelic, of which he possessed a huge collection. After school-time, Stevenson would spend hours with Sinclair and his volumes, and, at Sinclair's request, Stevenson 'improvised harmonizations of literally hundreds of these Irish tunes'. That activity seems, in a more exploratory fashion, to mirror his childhood accompanying of his father's singing; and it was surely valuable experience in the handling of Celtic folk-material, getting it into his ears and fingers, and assimilating it into his

---

3. Ronald Stevenson, 'MacLean: Musician manqué (and a composer's collaboration)', in *Sorley MacLean: Critical Essays*, ed. Raymond J. Ross and Joy Hendry (Edinburgh: Scottish Academic Press, 1986), p.177. Hereafter cited as 'MacLean'.

4. Ronald Stevenson, 'The Emergence of Scottish Music', in *Memoirs of a Modern Scotland*, ed. Karl Miller (London: Faber and Faber, 1970), p.189.

Stevenson near West Linton.

musical bloodstream. Later he became friends with the composer and musicologist Francis Collinson, the great authority of his generation on Scottish folk-music. It is certainly relevant to note that the School of Scottish Studies in Edinburgh, of which Collinson was a founder member, had begun its work in 1951, the year before Stevenson arrived there; and that it was during the 1950s that the remarkable modern revival of Scots folk music was getting under way.

From the later 1950s onwards, Stevenson began to make transcriptions and arrangements of Scots traditional tunes, either as songs, piano pieces, or for other media such as string orchestra. These included such perennial favourites of the BBC's Scottish Home Service as *A Rosebud by my Early Walk*, *John Anderson, my Jo*, and *The Birks o' Aberfeldy*. Though undertaken each for its own sake and eventually grouped into a series of *Scottish Folk-Music Settings* (an overall title that deliberately recalls the many *British Folk-Music Settings* of Percy Grainger, to whose memory Stevenson's are 'lovingly and reverently' dedicated), these sincerely affectionate miniature compositions acted as an unconscious fertilization for the Scottish side of Stevenson's musical personality.

The first of them, the song *Lang hae we pairted been* (1957; there is a later solo piano version), is touchingly symbolic of the composer's dawning realization that he had truly discovered his roots. Opening with an introduction marked 'like trumpets frae lang syne' (a very Graingeresque use of the vernacular), this short yet moving piece typically treats its noble tune contrapuntally, in a series of strict canonic textures climaxing in a 3-part canon by augmentation that John Ogdon once commented might have come from a page of Busoni's *Faust*. The haunting little piano-piece *From an old Pibroch*, mentioned earlier, is a simpler member of this group. A later setting in strict canonic style, *Hard is my Fate*, is of a tune Stevenson discovered in the collection of the fiddle-tune anthologizer and composer Captain Simon Fraser (1773–1852) of Knockie, Inverness-shire. Deeply moved by its expressive purity and evocation of the political tragedy of Scotland as experienced by the common people, Stevenson set it as a grave contrapuntal dialogue, in versions for solo piano and for violin with piano accompaniment. More elaborate is the *Ne'er Day Sang*, sketched in the late 1950s and later completed in several forms for solo piano, violin and piano, and string quartet. This is a treatment of an unaccompanied pentatonic melody which Stevenson encountered in William Sterling's Cantus Part-Book, dated 1639: he was fascinated by its wide vocal compass and large leaps, qualities he came to realize were highly characteristic of much Gaelic song.

Stevenson's circle of creative acquaintance in the 1950s was comprised more of artists and poets than of other composers. Not long after his arrival he became a member of the Scottish Arts Club, proposed by the painter Shand Hutchison — not to be confused with Ian Hutchinson, who in 1960 did an oil portrait of Stevenson entitled 'The Laughing Cavalier of the Café Royal'. From the first, he adored Edinburgh: favourite haunts included the walk to the summit of

Stevenson in the Café Royal, Edinburgh.

Arthur's Seat, often in the early morning, to see the (nowadays virtually extinguished) smokes of 'Auld Reekie'; and St Cuthbert's churchyard, where Thomas De Quincey's neglected grave became a frequent pausing-place for meditation. In this love-affair with his 'own Romantic city', he became an habitué of its famous pubs — the Café Royal and the numerous establishments of Rose Street (Edinburgh's 'Amber Mile'), such as Milne's Bar, the haunt of Scotland's aspiring poets, and the Abbotford. It was in the Abbotsford that Stevenson met Hector Maciver, and the poet Norman McCaig. At the Arts Club Stevenson became close friends with the painter John Maxwell — deeply interested in music (and, by happy coincidence, especially in the music of Busoni). Another good friend he made at this time was Manfred Gordon, who has since become a world-famous research chemist in the field of high polymers, and is a Gold Medallist of the Prague Academy of Sciences. He is also a Dantologist of the first rank whose researches into Dante as a scientist, and whose interpretation of the *Divina commedia* as a poetic, scientific and philosophical exploration of the origin of life, has deeply influenced Stevenson (who shares Busoni's reverence for Dante as the greatest of all poets). The friendship is celebrated in the *Variations on a Theme (Tema Ebraico) by Manfred Gordon*, which Stevenson composed for string quartet in 1977 to mark the scientist's sixtieth birthday. The distinguished physician John Guthrie — who also composed, and was long a composition-pupil of Stevenson's — was another firm friend made in those early years in Edinburgh; and through him Stevenson met Guthrie's friend and fellow New Zealander, the poet Sydney Goodsir Smith, who in Stevenson's opinion had more consummately mastered Scots as a poetic language than any other writer, including Hugh MacDiarmid.

Stevenson encountered MacDiarmid, or rather Chris Grieve, on a Borders-bound bus at Christmas 1956: a meeting that sparked a close and mutually enriching friendship, an artistic comradeship, that lasted until the poet's death in 1978. Stevenson visited the Grieves many times at their little farm-labourer's cottage at Candymill near Biggar, and the poet and his wife often visited the Stevensons. Undismayed by MacDiarmid's colossal egoism, Stevenson is

UNIVERSITY OF HOUSTON
MUSIC LIBRARY
106 FINE ARTS
HOUSTON, TEXAS 77204-4898

convinced he was the greatest genius he has ever met. His lyric and intellectual gifts, his breadth of culture and passionate nationalism, were all an inspiration to Stevenson on his own artistic path.

> He is the epic poet in his *Drunk Man* and *In Memoriam James Joyce*; lyric poet in *Sangschaw* and *Penny Wheep*; as erotic as any poet in *Wheesht, wheesht ye fule*; the tragedian in his translation of Rilke's *Requiem*, and grand comedian in *Crowdieknowe*; secular psalmist in his *Hymns to Lenin*; verbal Terpsichorean in his dance-song *I heard Christ sing*; and in *The Bonnie Broukit Bairn*, like Dante long ago, he cocks a cosmonaut's eye at the earth, years before Gagarin . . . : which poet alive has this range?[5]

Combative friendship blossomed into artistic collaboration, as Stevenson began to set to music many of MacDiarmid's poems — a process that continued for many years, concentrating on the later poetry. An especial stimulus — not to setting, but to musical emulation — was MacDiarmid's 'Vision of World Language' in *In Memoriam James Joyce*, a 100-page poem incorporating passages in twenty languages: a parallel (and political polar opposite) to the kind of grand synthesis of human history, universalized in its particulars, that Ezra Pound had attempted in his *Cantos*. Here was an inexhaustible source of ideas.

In 1962 Stevenson contributed an essay to the *MacDiarmid Festschrift* published to mark the poet's seventieth birthday. His title, 'MacDiarmid, Joyce and Busoni', typically and invigoratingly links three of the creative figures that have meant most to him in mutually illuminating comparisons intended as a sketch 'towards a music-aesthetic of literature'.

> These three artists form a somewhat incongruous and improbable and faintly unholy trinity. But their work in its inner core exists in symbiotic relationship, and, collectively, represents a philosophic eclecticism which is the reason, and not the excuse, for its being.[6]

---

5. Ronald Stevenson, 'MacDiarmid's Muses', in *The Age of MacDiarmid*, ed. P.H. Scott and A.C. Davis (Edinburgh: Mainstream Publishing, 1980), p.163.

6. Ronald Stevenson, 'MacDiarmid, Joyce and Busoni: Towards a Music-Aesthetic of Literature', in *Hugh MacDiarmid: a Festschrift*, ed. K.D. Duval and Sydney Goodsir Smith (Edinburgh: K.D. Duval, 1962), p.141. Hereafter cited as 'MJB'.

Stevenson's love of synthesis, of the coalescence of ideas, has seldom been more elegantly displayed than in this article whose nexus (Ezra Pound would have called it a Vortex) is the demonstration that the final portion of MacDiarmid's *In Memoriam James Joyce* encompasses a direct transcription into poetry, precisely analogous to a musical transcription from one instrument to another, of Busoni's visionary prose essay 'The Realm of Music'.

A major element in Stevenson's friendship with MacDiarmid was the poet's keen interest in — and decided views upon — music, both traditional and contemporary. He had written eloquently on the 'Great Music' of the highland bagpipe, the *Ceol Mor*, in his magnificent *Lament for the Great Music* and in his book on *The Islands of Scotland*; and was aware of (and quoting) composers such as Schoenberg and Satie in the 1920s, and Henry Cowell and Skalkottas in the 1950s, long before they impinged on the general musical consciousness of Britain. Among MacDiarmid's composer friends were several who represented vivid and even exotic alternatives to the current orthodoxies of classical music, none more so than the almost legendary Kaikhosru Shapurji Sorabji (?1892-1988). British-born of a Parsi father and a Spanish-Sicilian mother, Sorabji — who had been a member of the Van Dieren-Warlock circle in the London of the 1920s, and whose early works were praised by Busoni — has been a figure of fascination to discriminating musicians, and especially pianists, ever since. As a writer on music he was an inimitably colourful and combative stylist; as a composer he had written a wealth of music, principally for piano, of supra-transcendental technical difficulty and (in many works) of unprecedented length. Some of it was printed and available; but after a pianist's particularly poor performance of one piece in 1936, Sorabji had withheld all further rights of public performance, so for the space of a generation his works had become an unattainable peak of pianism, tantalizingly extraordinary on the printed page, studied by exceptionally brave piano virtuosi in the privacy of their homes.

Stevenson already knew of Sorabji, of course: but MacDiarmid knew Sorabji personally — indeed, he was the dedicatee of the most gigantic and visually extraordinary of all Sorabji's published works,

Stevenson and Hugh MacDiarmid, on the occasion of MacDiarmid's 75th birthday.

the *Opus clavicembalisticum* (1930): an approximately four-hour, three-part, twelve-movement solo piano fantasia (taking the general conception of Busoni's monumental *Fantasia contrappuntistica* as a mere point of departure) that mingles gigantesque examples of polyphonic forms such as fugue, passacaglia, theme and variations, with a much more impressionistic, deliquescent, arabesque-like style.

Sorabji had given *Opus clavicembalisticum* its première in Glasgow in 1930; the work was not to be heard again entire in the British Isles until 1988 (Sorabji, living a reclusive existence in Dorset, began in the 1970s to permit selected pianists to play his music again), when John Ogdon performed it in London, a rendering that must rank among the historic achievements of 20th-century pianism. But this was not the first time that Ogdon, who had already been fascinated by Sorabji's music for years, had played the work. In 1959, Stevenson had arranged for him to give a very special private performance — in the Stevensons' sitting-room in West Linton, in the presence of MacDiarmid, the work's dedicatee. On that occasion Ogdon, MacDiarmid, and Stevenson recorded a conversation about the work, and resolved to collaborate on a book on Sorabji. Although they all duly wrote their contributions, only MacDiarmid's portion of the project found its way readily into print — in his autobiographical volume *The Company I've Kept* (1966), which also included a transcript of the three-cornered conversation. But the core of the collaboration was Stevenson's detailed analysis of *Opus clavicembalisticum*.[7] In the event, Stevenson found himself less impressed by Sorabji's capacities as a writer of fugue (of which O.C., as it is known to its friends, contains four increasingly Brobdingnagian examples) than by his oriental gift for arabesque, involute decoration and fioriture, the instinctive coalescence of the aesthetic ideals of East and West. Here was a clue to his own future path.

---

7. This was only finally published, as was John Ogdon's essay on Sorabji and Herman Melville, and Stevenson's introductory tribute to Sorabji, 'A Zoroastrian Musician in Dorset', as part of the booklet accompanying Ogdon's compact disc recording of the work, issued by Altarus Records in May 1989.

It was from Sorabji's writings, in his essay-collection *Mi contra Fa*, that Stevenson had first become aware of one Scottish composer whose art-music rivalled the most advanced of his European contemporaries while retaining an awareness of native Scots folk-traditions: the Hawick-born songwriter Francis George Scott (1880-1958), whose nearly one hundred *Scottish Lyrics* and other songs, issued between 1922 and 1949, proclaimed a mastery of his medium that Sorabji had not hesitated to rank with the best of Hugo Wolf. It was in Book III of *Scottish Lyrics* (published 1934) — as epoch-making a collection in its national context as MacDiarmid's *Sangschaw*, and still far less celebrated — that Scottish art-music had finally confronted the 20th century. In these songs, mostly composed in the 1920s, Scott had forged a powerfully individual language: rooted in Scottish speech-rhythm, folk-song, fiddle music, Border ballads, pub songs and pibroch; influenced to some extent by Mussorgsky and Debussy (reflecting his studies in Paris with Roger-Ducasse), while displaying a creative assimilation of Schoenbergian free chromaticism and of Bartók's dissonant and essentialized treatments of folk materials. At once earthy and mystical, this extraordinary feat of synthesis made for a versatile song-writing style that lifted even Scott's slightest productions clean out of the kailyard. Though his output is certainly uneven in quality, many of his settings of Robert Burns and Hugh MacDiarmid number among the finest art-songs ever produced by a Scottish composer.

Stevenson's interest in Scott received a fresh impetus from MacDiarmid himself, for the poet and composer had long maintained a close, almost symbiotic friendship: Scott, the dedicatee of *A Drunk Man Looks at the Thistle*, had taught the boy Chris Grieve as a schoolmaster in Langholm, and had been one of the shrewdest and most constructive critics of his poetry. MacDiarmid once described him as 'blazing with spiritual energy'. A year before Stevenson first met MacDiarmid, the poet had published a fiercely polemical essay on the occasion of his composer's seventy-fifth birthday, averring that 'there is no comparison between Scott and any other composer Scotland has ever produced; he stands on a plane of his own, immeasurably removed from theirs'. Scott, a cantankerous and not unembittered man impatient with the compromises required to promote his songs, had nevertheless remained a marginalized figure on the Scottish musical scene. Stevenson, however, was quick to recognize in him a prophet of the kind of Scottish music he himself wished to create, and found his example a precious stimulus to achievement. The two composers never met: by the mid-1950s Scott had ceased to compose and had retreated into crusty seclusion. But Stevenson studied his music closely, transcribed several of the songs as solo piano pieces, introduced some of them at Dartington Hall in 1956, and has since dedicatedly performed his works, becoming one of the most enthusiastic and discriminating advocates for this isolated genius of Scottish music.

On 7 November 1958, Stevenson flew to Dublin to give a recital; opening a newspaper on the plane, he read that F.G. Scott had died the previous day. Deeply moved, he began then and there, far above the Irish Sea, the first sketch of what became *Keening Sang for a Makar (In Memoriam Francis George Scott)*. Completed the following year, this plangently evocative piano composition is both a distillation and expansion of the motivic methods Stevenson had explored in the studies contained in the *20th-Century Music Diary*. The dead composer's initials, FGS, yield a 3-note shape, F-G-E flat — a very 'Scottish' shape, with its wide, aspiring leap to the flattened seventh, that occurs already, note for note, in the *Ne'erday Sang*. In the *Keening Sang* these notes are the kernel from which the whole work springs: indeed, to begin with, the music uses just those pitches, both melodically and harmonically, along with a chromaticized variant, F-G flat-E natural. From this extremely limited thematic kernel Stevenson's invention puts forth roots and spreads its branches to embrace a wide harmonic spectrum — by way of the tritone figure F-B, and an ethereal quotation from one of Scott's greatest songs, the magnificently timeless, 'pibroch-style' Jean Lang setting *St. Brendan's Graveyard: Isle of Barra* (1934). The ideas move through extreme chromaticism, Hebridean pentatony, Schoenbergian fourth-chords, and in a *fortissississimo* climax, the searing dissonance of 10-note 'cluster' harmonies. Finally the F-G-S motif develops into a bardic funeral march, redolent of ancient epic and distant mountain landscapes.

The *Keening Sang for a Makar* remains 'essential Stevenson', one of his most profoundly characteristic and impressive piano pieces (in 1963 he made a version for full orchestra, never yet performed). In its drastic motivic economy, however, it was also prophetic of a much vaster work which would soon be based on a different set of composer-initials. Stevenson had long admired the work of the contemporary Soviet master, Dmitri Shostakovich, both as a modern symphonist and peerless contrapuntist (for instance in his *24 Preludes and Fugues* for piano), and as the prime representative of a living national tradition of Russian music, extending from the basis of the deeply humane and folk-centred art of Mussorgsky. The German spelling of the composer's name, 'D. Schostakowich', yields the monogram 'DSCH', which also spells a four-note musical motif, just as 'BACH' does. Shostakovich himself made use of this figure as a kind of musical signature in several of his works, notably his Tenth Symphony and Eighth String Quartet.

This figure fascinated Stevenson, as Busoni's 'Clavis Astartis Magica' had. With its introverted chromaticism, its rising and falling semitones mirroring each other and yet spanning the diatonic interval of the major third, it seemed to enshrine the harmonic and melodic character of his own music. Like the atomic nucleus whose splitting releases the power of the sun, it was to provide him with the basis for a staggering creative feat. On Christmas Eve, 1960, Stevenson began sketching some passacaglia variations, using DSCH as an immutable ground bass. Conceived at first as pure polyphony with no especial instrumentation in mind, the initial variations (two pages' worth, at one sitting) rapidly opened up a kaleidoscope of possibilities, and the work began to take on an urgent life of its own, soon expanding root and branch to formidable dimensions.

James Joyce, writing the section *Anna Livia Plurabelle* in his *Finnegans Wake*, began by weaving a few names of rivers into his prose-poem and went on piling up river-names until the text was a torrent of over 500 of them. That is something like how I wrote my *Passacaglia.* I went on piling up variations over that ground bass until they grew into hundreds. I don't know how many hundreds: I've never counted them. I felt the nature of the work was 'aqueous' — it should flow. For that reason it should be in one movement. And in the flow should be other forms, similar to what geologists call 'aqueous rocks'.[8]

Stevenson found himself launched on a year-and-a-quarter of sustained creative effort, whose result, completed on 18 May 1962, was the work by which he has become most widely known: the *Passacaglia on DSCH* for solo piano. This eighty-minute single movement, of Sorabjian length but quite un-Sorabjian thematic and contrapuntal rigour, is quite simply one of the supreme summits of 20th-century piano literature, and as such is discussed in detail in the next chapter. That summer, when 'D.Sch' himself visited Edinburgh as a guest of the Edinburgh International Festival, Stevenson presented Shostakovich with a copy of the score, at a reception chaired by Hugh MacDiarmid.

It was on that very day that MacDiarmid suggested to Stevenson the idea of applying the *Passacaglia's* multi-variational approach to perhaps the greatest masterpiece of Gaelic poetry, *The Praise of Ben Dorain*, by Duncan Bàn MacIntyre (1724–1808), in MacDiarmid's own verse translation. Stevenson set to work at once, on a huge setting for double chorus and orchestra, envisaged at first as a choral symphony, though that designation was later dropped. The project was to be worked upon at intervals for more than a decade, being completed (as a continuous short score draft) in the early 1970s. But this counterpart and complement to the *Passacaglia* (Stevenson estimates the duration of its single movement at about 50 minutes) has remained unheard; indeed, it has not progressed to a full score. As someone who depends upon his composing and playing for his livelihood, Stevenson can hardly afford to squander the many months, perhaps years, necessary to construct a very large orchestral full score and parts in the absence of the commission and firm commitment to a performance which would justify the labour. *Ben Dorain* remains therefore the 'great unknown' in his voluminous output: but also, clearly, one of its central achievements.

---

8. 'Ronald Stevenson writes about his *Passacaglia on DSCH*', *The Listener*, 9 October 1969, p.494.

In preparing for this book there has been no opportunity for me to study *Ben Dorain* at first hand; and as the work is as yet unheard, it seems appropriate to quote (with the author's kind permission) a brief and also hitherto unpublished description of it by the young Scots poet and linguist James Reid-Baxter.[9]

[The work] is in actual fact a gigantic 'pibroch', for that is exactly what the poem itself is. It begins with an *urlar* or slow ground, the splendour of the mountain itself, ablaze with light, and then in ever more complex variations explores this haunt of the wild deer with plentiful and accurate descriptions of the animals themselves. For Donnchadh Ban Mac-an-t-Saòir was a game-keeper, and his masterpiece culminates in the hunting of the deer, which Stevenson sets as a gigantic and exultant fast fugue of quite breathtaking exhilaration. Into the work's fabric the composer has woven many of the folksongs associated with the mountain, and the singing text employs parts of the Gaelic original as well as MacDiarmid's paraphrase. This work Stevenson regards as a *summa*. Everything he has done since 1962 may be regarded as a side-study.

How can a man like Stevenson set hunting poetry? In *Ben Dorain*, the deer are not the prey, but the *quarry*, from Latin *quaerere*, to seek, to desire, cf. Spanish *querer*, to love. What Stevenson's hunters are seeking out on the slopes of the mountain, with all their skill, all their love and understanding of the quarry, is the elusive soul of Scotland, the essence of that conjunction of race and place which is a nation.

---

9. From an article, 'Stevenson and Scotland', written in 1983, intended for — but withdrawn from — a forthcoming symposium to be published by Toccata Press.

Stevenson presenting his Passacaglia on DSCH *to Shostakovich.*

4

PASSACAGLIA

> ...brooding over all the world history of the dance,
> Review with the mind's eye all the forms,
> Passecaille, chaconne, sarabande ...

> Hugh MacDiarmid
> *In Memoriam James Joyce*

IN his address to Shostakovich, when he presented the Soviet master with a bound copy of the manuscript of *Passacaglia on DSCH*,[1] Stevenson averred that:

the work is written in an international (but not cosmopolitan) spirit, and includes, within the larger framework, dances from many countries. It also contains a long drum-like passage marked 'to emergent Africa'. Another section is based on speech-intonation associated with the classical slogan of 1917: PEACE, BREAD AND THE LAND. Yet another passage was inspired by the idea of the Soviet hammer beating the Nazi swastika into a sickle. The idea of the hammer is, of course, inherent in the mechanism of the piano; and though music is (mercifully) powerless to paint a swastika, it can certainly suggest the mechanistic devilry and brutality of which the crooked cross is but the symbol. As contrast to that passage, but linked with it, is another in which I have combined the motif DSCH with the time-honoured motif BACH; as a symbol that Russian and German and the whole of mankind can and will live as brothers in harmony and peace. The work contains a triple fugue, with the ground bass ever present. The third theme of the triple fugue is the Dies Irae, which I have expressly marked: in memoriam the six million Jews. The whole work is consummated in a final series of variations marked *adagissimo*. In one passage of this section I

---

1. It lacked at this stage the Pibroch, 'Lament for the Children', not composed until the day of the première in December 1963; and the section 'To Emergent Africa' was to be revised in the light of his experiences on that continent.

Stevenson listens as John Ogdon performs Sorabji's Opus
Clavicembalisticum, *1959.*

have used the expression *'con un senso di spazio quasi gagarinesco'* (as though with Gagarin's[2] perception of space).

It was his most all-embracing achievement to date, forging a monumental, indeed monolithic, unity out of the greatest possible diversity of material and background: a landmark not only of his creative development, but in the history of the piano. He had written possibly the longest continuous movement in piano literature, with a playing-time of about eighty minutes; and in rendering homage to the composer whose acronym is enshrined in its every bar, he drew upon the potential of many diverse musical cultures.

The passacaglia form has roots in the dance, specifically a triple-time Spanish dance of seductive display (the name is an Italianization of the Spanish *pasar calle*, to walk the street). From Renaissance times the associations of 'display' had caused composers to develop this dance into a bravura instrumental composition upon a ground — that is, an unchanging tune, played throughout, usually (but not invariably) in the bass, which is decorated by the free variation of the other parts. (Passacaglia is closely related to the chaconne, where the ground always remains in the bass.) In the Baroque era it attained popularity as a vehicle for showing off compositional skill; there are notable examples by Handel, Purcell (three of whose 'Grounds' Stevenson had transcribed in the 1950s for piano, for violin, and for guitar), and pre-eminently Bach. The effect of this 'ancient' form can be found in many of Beethoven's variation works, but it was Brahms who really revived it in the late 19th century: most potently in his Fourth Symphony, whose finale is a strict passacaglia of 35 variations on a theme derived from Bach. Thereafter passacaglia was employed as a particularly demanding species of variation by many composers — among them Max Reger, Schoenberg, Webern, Walton, and Shostakovich (for instance in his opera *Lady Macbeth of Mtsensk*, and his First Violin Concerto).

None of these former examples, however, approaches the immensity of Stevenson's conception, which is virtually a synthesis,

---

2. Yuri Gagarin, the first man in space, had orbited the Earth in 1961, while Stevenson was at work on his composition.

within one form, of the entire piano repertoire. Much of his *Passacaglia* is in fact performable by pianists of average ability, though there are some sections (such as the central Études) only accessible to a transcendentally virtuosic technique. But the piece exacts an unremitting toll on the performer's stamina, imposing its most extreme demands for absolute control of touch, tempo, and texture about seventy minutes in — *after* the pulverising triple fugue which a lesser composer would have made the work's culmination. Yet far more is asked throughout than mere muscle power, prestidigitation, grasp of large structure, and skill in polyphonic playing. Stevenson requires vision, feeling for narrative, love of variety and curious detail for its own sake, and the ability to think about musical issues in their human context.

He derives the 'ground' of his *Passacaglia* from the letters 'D.Sch', the initials of Shostakovich's name in German orthography (German being the second of music's three great *linguae francae*, of which Italian is the first and French only the third), turned into the German nomenclature of musical notes to form a figure of four pitches D, E-flat ('Es'), C, and B-natural:

Example 3

Stevenson takes this four-note cell, repeats it with octave trans-positions, and then plays it in retrograde, to produce a seven-bar theme that serves him as 'ground' throughout his entire work.

Example 4

Poster announcing a performance of the Passacaglia on DSCH *in Sofia, 1968.*

This always appears at the same relative pitch, no matter how far the movement of the surrounding parts may cause the music to range across the field of other tonalities. Although 'DSCH' will only fit diatonically into the key of C minor, Stevenson centres his work on D minor (with a persistent and very Russian-sounding flattened second), reserving C minor for a group of variations two-thirds of the way through.

It is a necessary paradox of passacaglia form that a large, 'seamless', continuous movement is produced from the multitudinous separate building-blocks demarcated by the repetitions of the ground. Stevenson's sovereign handling of his *Passacaglia's* enormous structure probably rests, by a fine parallel paradox, on his love of musical miniatures: each variation in this work is in effect a tiny composition in its own right. However, the seven-bar structure of Stevenson's theme always implies an eighth bar — the first of the next variation — to complete it, producing an onward impetus that is intensified by the cadential motion of the *cancrizans* figure in bar 7. Thus, each variation *requires* the next, and the music unfolds under an irresistible impetus.

It is an astonishing tribute to Stevenson's powers of invention that, despite the many-hundredfold repetitions of the 7-bar formula, the listener's interest is held by a pianistic invention as glittering as the eye of Coleridge's Ancient Mariner. And complementing this is a sheer mastery of musical architecture, unerring in its placing of light and shade, drama and humour, lyricism and improvissatory fantasy, meditative episode and volcanic climax, build-up and relaxation of tension. The result is a re-structuring of the sense of time. The Canadian musicologist Paul Rapoport, comparing Stevenson's achievement to Proust's labyrinthine novel-sequence *À la recherche du temps perdu*, has written, of the *Passacaglia's* eighty-minute duration:

> In the experiencing of this composition, clock time is unreal. Real musical time, intense and immanent in such an undertaking, is very different. It is quite possible to feel, after hearing the *Passacaglia*, that it is much shorter than its stated duration, and, after hearing it a few times and thinking about it for a while, that it is much longer.[3]

The individual variations combine to produce large structural units which themselves articulate the successive, contrasting stages of Stevenson's huge single movement. His ground-plan for the *Passacaglia* (see illustration) is an intricate architectural design recalling the monumental precedents of Busoni's *Fantasia Contrappuntistica* and Sorabji's *Opus Clavicembalisticum*, to both of which Stevenson's work is a creative response (and, in the case of the Sorabji, something of a critique). But these themselves are only two relatively recent examples from a grand tradition of quasi-encyclopaedic contrapuntal and/or variation works, to which the *Passacaglia on DSCH* is the latest addition. Equally relevant are the *24 Preludes and Fugues* of Shostakovich himself, Bach's *Goldberg Variations* and *Art of Fugue*, and, perhaps closest of all in spirit, the *Diabelli Variations* of Beethoven, with its canonic variations, beatific minuet and stupefying culminatory fugue.

---

3. Sleeve-note for Stevenson's second disc recording of the *Passacaglia*, for Altarus Records.

What sets Stevenson's work apart from these masterpieces of the European tradition are, first, its extension of piano technique to produce unusual sonorities by unorthodox means, often directly on the strings — glissandi around silently-depressed keys, note-clusters, fingernail glissandi on the strings, slapping the bass strings with the palm of the hand to create 'drum' effects. Second, and much more important, is its 'global' range of reference. This is most prominently displayed in the tumultuous 'African drumming' section; and in the deeply moving Pibroch variation, which is essentially a transcription of the *urlar* of the 17th-century pibroch lament, *Cumha na Cloinne* (Lament for the Children), composed after the death of his own sons by Patrick Mor MacCrimmon, perhaps the greatest member of the celebrated piping family long associated with Dunvegan in Skye. The plangent clashing of major and minor thirds here suggests the microtonal inflections of the bagpipe scale.

Example 5

The 'global' vision also informs the national characters of the dance suite that occurs fairly early in the work, notably the heroic, Chopinesque revolutionary Polonaise; such later episodes as the Spanish Fandango; and, most extensively, in the Russian enclave of the second part, with its musical equivalent of an Eisenstein crowd-scene, its Shostakovichian march, and the 'Peace, Bread and the Land' variations, built (above the ground) on a theme reflecting the speech-rhythm of the Russian slogan *Mir Khleb i Zemlya*. This peaceful coexistence of 'regional' styles is one secret of the work's unflagging diversity, but also points towards a larger unity than any that has been available to music before the present century. The *Passacaglia* is Stevenson's first, almost unconscious approach to the ideal of 'World Music' that he has pursued in later years.

Nonetheless, the climactic third part is essentially and sometimes darkly European in orientation, largely occupied as it is by a colossal triple fugue over the still-unexhausted ground (in itself an innovation in fugal form). The first of its three successive subjects is a spiky theme containing eleven of the twelve chromatic notes. The fact that the second subject, Bach's signature B-A-C-H, is closely akin to Shostakovich's D-S-C-H, leads to a rare accord between them when they conjoin in the grave slow fugal writing that is the work's most vivid evocation of Busoni's *Fantasia Contrappuntistica*. The shape of the third subject, the 'Dies Irae' plainchant, establishes relationships to both these motifs, and turns the final portion of the fugue into a galvanic Lisztian *Totentanz* where eventually all three fugue subjects are heard in contrapuntal combination with the ground.

One of the disconcerting aspects of the *Passacaglia* is Stevenson's capacity to pile Pelion upon Ossa and convince his hearers that that is where it belongs. Rather than diminishing towards the end, his powers of invention seem, on the contrary, to increase. The most intense and impressive music in the entire composition comes *after* the fugue, in the final *adagissimo* variations, which are worked out on the principle of Baroque 'doubles' — very slow, and building remorselessly from a sculptured simplicity, by way of the 'Gagarin-

Example 6

esque' sense of space, to a vast agglomerative climax that is truly the crown of all that has preceded it.

If nuclear or environmental Armageddon were indeed to wipe out human civilization, and one copy of one work by Ronald Stevenson were to be all that survived the disaster to show (musically literate) explorers from another solar system what one 20th-century composer was capable of, that work would have to be the *Passacaglia*. It by no means contains all of him, but no other single piece encompasses so much of his responses to tradition and cultural diversity. Even now, over 25 years since its completion, it remains the cornerstone of his achievement.

5

WORLD MUSIC

The true unity of languages is not an Esperanto or Volapuk or everyone speaking French, not a single language, but an all-embracing language, an interpenetration of all languages.

Vladimir Solovyof
(Russian poet, philosopher and theologian, 1853–1900:
quoted by Hugh MacDiarmid in the epigraph to
In Memoriam James Joyce)

STEVENSON'S *Passacaglia* was essentially complete in 1962. In March 1963 he left his teaching job in Broughton, having been invited by Professor Erik Chisholm, Head of Music at Cape Town University, to join his staff as a Senior Lecturer in Music. Chisholm (1904–65), also a Scot, had been a longtime sparring partner of Sorabji, F.G. Scott, and MacDiarmid, and was himself a mettlesome composer. Not knowing when he might next be in Europe, Stevenson travelled first to East Germany, pursuing his researches on Busoni at the East Berlin Stadtsbibliothek, which possesses the largest collection of Busoni manuscripts. Then he and his family made the 6,000-mile sea voyage to the southern tip of Africa.

It was at Cape Town University, where he taught composition and piano, that Stevenson gave the *Passacaglia* its world première, in the University's Hiddinghe Hall on 10 December 1963. Shortly before the performance, he went to the shanty-town of Nyanga, a Bantu settlement near Cape Town 'surrounded by barbed wire, buzzed a few times a day by helicopter', to adjudicate a singing competition of black children. Crossing a piece of waste ground during this visit, he came across a solitary Bantu man, naked apart from a loincloth, playing 15 drums arranged round him in a semi-circle: a real tribal virtuoso. Stevenson was astounded at his rhythmic artistry.

Part of [the *Passacaglia*] had been inspired by the idea of emergent Africa: it was written in drum rhythms, beginning in a deep register and gradually rising into the treble.

After the experience of hearing the tribal drummer, I felt very dissatisfied with my work. I remember going toward the piano in the main hall of the University (it was an eight-foot Petroff grand, a Czech instrument which had been imported into South Africa because of the enthusiasm of a number of music-lovers in Cape Town after hearing Michelangeli play his own Petroff). When I approached that piano, very dissatisfied with what I had composed, I depressed the right pedal and gently struck the bass strings. The sound of the 32-foot C on this Petroff grand suggested the possibility of striking the lower strings directly to evoke the sound I had heard. . . .

This was not a gimmick that began as a kind of Cageian direct-contact tactic on the strings. It began from an aural experience of hearing the African drummer and then asking, how can I do that? How can I evoke those sounds?. . . I subsequently discovered that if one began by touching the strings — just tapping with the fingertips — later on using the palm of the hand and finally at the height of the *crescendo* the heel of the hand, quite different sonorities could be obtained.[1]

Thus Stevenson re-cast the 'Emergent Africa' section of the *Passacaglia* into the form we know today, with the percussive fusillade of on-string effects which makes it one of the work's most dumbfounding events. And it was on the day of the première itself that he finally added the pibroch, 'Lament for the Children', suddenly realizing that in this vast work with its evocations of African, Russian, Spanish, and other idioms, there was no specifically Scottish element. Indeed, Scotland was clearly much in Stevenson's mind during his South African sojourn. In early 1964, shortly after the *Passacaglia* première, he composed a whole series of songs to MacDiarmid's lyrics — some of his finest and most deeply-felt, such as *The Bobbin-Winder*, *The Skeleton of the Future*, *Coronach for the End of the World*, and *The last Trump*.

After the première of the *Passacaglia*, which created a great impression, Stevenson was awarded a grant by the University which enabled him to record it in a limited-edition 2-record set of 100 signed copies. But in the winter of 1964–65, fundamentally unhappy

---

1. Composer's Anthology, pp.749–50.

with his position in South Africa, Stevenson resigned his post at Cape Town, and returned with his family to West Linton. He had resolved not to resume schoolteaching but to devote himself to composing, writing and piano-playing. No engagement had yet been arranged except a Busoni Centenary recital-tour of British universities in 1966, so 1965 was a very difficult year. ('We lived on soup, mainly.') Creatively, 1965-66 proved a time for taking stock, a process symbolized by a whole crop of *Scottish Folk-Music Settings*, by the composition of the orchestral *Scots Dance Toccata* — an uproarious and instrumentally virtuosic showpiece based on tunes from the *Repository* of the great 18th-century fiddler-composer Niel Gow — and by a return to his teenage settings of Blake's *Songs of Innocence*, now finally rewritten as a cycle requiring four solo voices (soprano, alto, tenor, and bass) with flute and string quintet, transforming it into a major example of vocal chamber music.

But the sense of widened horizons imparted by the South African experience was not lost, and manifested itself in several 'folksong suites' for piano or piano duet, drawing upon the traditional musics of various non-European countries, among them China and Ghana. At the same time, the 'Gagarinesque' sense of space — the widest horizon of all — invoked at the close of the *Passacaglia*, was heard again in the first of four songs to poems by the young Edinburgh poet Alan Bold (a pupil of Stevenson's at Broughton in the 1950s). *Voskhod over Edinburgh*, a striking song even among Stevenson's vast vocal output, reflects, with a sure command of contrasted musical idioms both mysterious and popular, the contemporary excitement for spaceflight as seen in the passing of a Russian spaceship as a small brilliant star over Edinburgh's slum tenements. Its evocation of physical — and metaphysical — heights and depths would soon be applied in a very different vocal work, in Gaelic.

In 1966-67 Stevenson's public career took a marked turn for the better. Principally this was due to the *Passacaglia on DSCH*, whose first UK performances and broadcast, commercial publication, and recording, provided a high-profile demonstration of his prowess as composer and pianist and led to widespread recognition. In 1966 he received an award from the Arts Council of Great Britain to allow him to continue work on the *Ben Dorain* project. Stevenson himself gave the *Passacaglia* its European première in Halle University (GDR), on 6 June 1966, during a memorable trip to East Germany that took in Leipzig, Weimar (where he played on Liszt's piano), and the shattering emotional experience of visiting the museum at the Nazi death-camp of Buchenwald. The East German tour had been partly arranged through the good offices of the veteran British Marxist composer and master contrapuntist Alan Bush, who had studied in Germany in 1929-31 and had known Bertolt Brecht and his great musical collaborator Hanns Eisler. Stevenson's close friendship with Bush dates from the early 1960s (he wrote a major article about his compositions for the November 1964 issue of *Music Review*), and continues to the present day. ('A very significant figure in my life — I've never known a more sterling character among all my comrades-in-art.') Bush, with his many Eastern European contacts, was to be instrumental in enabling Stevenson to travel and perform on several occasions beyond the 'Iron Curtain', not only in East Germany but in Bulgaria and the USSR, where he met Shostakovich again.

Stevenson was also great friends with another distinguished British Marxist composer, Bernard Stevens (1916-83), who taught at the Royal College of Music in London. Quite apart from their politics, Bush's and Stevens's brand of highly contrapuntal, craftsmanly, and tonally-oriented music had served to place them somewhat outside the mainstream of the British music of their time, since they conformed neither to the traditional image of the British composer as primarily a pastoral mystic, nor to the post-Webernian serial orthodoxies then occupying the attentions of the current avant-garde. But Stevenson was drawn to both of them as human beings and by powerful musical affinities, recognizing the strong and timeless virtues of their unfashionable approach to their craft. Their example encouraged him in his own work.

At the 1966 Aldeburgh Festival (where Ogdon gave the *Passacaglia* its UK public première), an old friendship was renewed when Stevenson met Percy Grainger's widow, Ella. In the long term, this led to several visits and recitals at the Grainger House in White Plains, New York State; more immediately, Stevenson was invited to compile and arrange a selection of Grainger's works that could be played by children. The result was *The Young Pianist's Grainger*, published the following year by Schott, and a model of how to set out a teaching album for young players. Stevenson's interest in music for children had already produced his own little Scots keyboard suite, *A Wheen Tunes for Bairns Tae Spiel*, and a pair of waltzes, *Valse Garbo and Valse Charlot*, envisaged as 'cigarette-card portraits' of famous film-stars; he was later to produce a companion volume to the Grainger selection, *The Young Pianist's Delius*.

In early 1967 Stevenson broadcast on his music and aesthetic in the BBC Radio 3 series 'Composer's Portrait'. His roundly-declared commitment to Scottish music elicited a letter from W. Grant Kidd,

The poet Sorley MacLean.

conductor of the Greenock Gaelic Choir, asking if this extended to *Gaelic* music, and if Stevenson would be willing to write a choral work, on Gaelic texts, for his choir. Stevenson was in fact quite heavily involved in choral music at the time. Not only was *Ben Dorain* a fundamentally choral composition, but several important pieces of the later 1960s are for chorus. We might instance a stark, defiant part-song to words by Emily Brontë, *No Coward Soul is Mine* (1966); the *Mediaeval Scottish Triptych* (1967), memorably setting words by John Barbour, Blind Harry the Minstrel, and the anonymous Lament on the Death of King Alexander III; and, slightly later, the *Ballatis of Luve* (1971), a madrigal cycle for vocal quartet and lute to poems by the 16th-century Lallans poet, Alexander Scott. After due consideration, he accepted the commission, choosing three poems from the collection *Dain do Eimhir* (1943) by Scotland's leading Gaelic poet of the 20th century, Sorley MacLean.

Stevenson's cycle, composed in 1968, carries his own Gaelic title, *Anns an Airde, as an Doimhne* (In the Heights, from the Depths). Its first movement is a paean to the landscape of the Scottish Highlands, full of resonant open-air sonorities and vigorous imitation of Gaelic 'mouth-music' (*puirt a beul*); its last a kind of tranced cosmic elegy, contrasting the 'gold-sieve of a million stars,/ cold, distant, blazing, splendid,/ silent and callous in their course', with the true quickening of soul produced by the 'naked universe of love' which the poet sees in his beloved's face.[2] Between these comes one of Stevenson's most piercing examples of simple, lyrical writing. In 'Calbharaigh' (Calvary), solo voices are borne upon hummed background harmonies in an infinitely tender lament for the blighted lives lived out in Lowland city slums:

> My een are nae on Calvary
> or the Bethlehem they praise,
> But on shitten backlands in Glasga toun
> whaur growan life decays. . . .[3]

---

2. Quotations from the translation by Iain Crichton Smith, *Poems to Eimhir* (London: Gollancz, 1971).

3. Scots metrical translation by Douglas Young.

The experience of working on this Gaelic choral cycle brought Stevenson the friendship of Sorley MacLean himself; he visited the poet at his home in Plockton, and listened to his daughter singing songs handed down from Sorley's grandmother, Mary MacLean.

> The poet, who has described himself as a musician *manqué*, evidently treasured every phrase, each note, all the nuances of these folksongs from Skye, Kintail and Lochalsh, whose preservation, in some cases, was unique to the MacLean family. These songs are the *fons et origo* of the phenomenon of MacLean, the musician-in-words. In a literary *milieu* in which verbal music has been virtually silenced ... MacLean is a lone exemplar of the art of the singing word.[4]

Stevenson later also stayed with MacLean in Skye. In the later '60s and '70s his summer holidays were often spent in the Hebrides, sometimes on South Uist, whose songs are celebrated in his *A South Uist (Hebridean) Folksong Suite* (1969), or on Tiree. It was during these Hebridean forays that Stevenson really began to study the Great Music (*Ceol Mor*) of the Highland bagpipe at first hand, talking and listening to pipers in their crofts. On Tiree in 1967 he met another MacLean, the piper Calum MacLean of Salum Bay, known locally as 'Calum Salum', and renowned for a feat worthy of the many Celtic legends about 'The People of the Sea': by playing slow airs on his bagpipes by the shore, he could conjure the seals out of the water. Stevenson was inspired to compose his own pibroch for pipes[5] — *Calum Salum's Salute to the Seals*.

Later, that pibroch became the starting-point for a new piano-piece, *Chorale-Pibroch for Sorley MacLean*, a bracing and resplendent work that mingles the traditional resonant sonorities of drone fifths, and passages in 'Scotch Psalm' idiom, with Stevenson's characteristic inside-of-piano sonorities, such as glissandi directly on the strings and delicately plucked strings infiltrating a more orthodox keyboard texture. The *Chorale-Pibroch* formed a natural companion-piece to

---

4. MacLean, p.178.

5. Probably only the second ever written by a non-piper (the first was by Francis Collinson).

another piano composition. The *Heroic Song for Hugh MacDiarmid*, commissioned by the BBC to mark the poet's 75th birthday in 1967, evokes MacDiarmid's (and Stevenson's) beloved Border hill-country with imitations of echoing horns in the hills, and a kaleidoscopic succession of moods typical of the poet, ranging from *Maestoso, irato* (Majestically angry) to a nobly 'Bardic' *Andante*, via an unmistakable impersonation of his cackling mirth. Stevenson finally grouped this *Heroic Song* together with the *Chorale-Pibroch* and the earlier *Keening Sang for a Makar*, to form *A 20th-Century Scottish Triptych* – a multiform homage to three of Scotland's greatest creative artists of recent times which itself encapsulates some of Stevenson's finest music.

His association with MacDiarmid remained as close as ever, and at the very beginning of the 1970s gave rise to two major song-cycles for tenor and piano to MacDiarmid texts. *Border Boyhood* (1970), commissioned by Peter Pears for the Aldeburgh Festival, and premièred there by Pears and Stevenson in 1971, is largely based on prose passages from an autobiographical essay, 'Growing up in Langholm', which MacDiarmid contributed to *Memoirs of a Modern Scotland* (1970), the symposium in memory of Hector MacIver for which Stevenson wrote his article 'The Emergence of Scottish Music'. The cycle is Stevenson's most elaborate apostrophe of the natural beauty and poetry of the Scottish Borders, and nowhere more so than in the florid, ecstatically exfoliating textures of the third song, 'A Celebration of Colour'. The final item, 'The Nook of the Night Paths', is in a very unusual, perhaps unparalleled form for a song, being an elaborate fugue that involves voice as well as piano; indeed, at one point the singer provides his own two-part counterpoint as his part splits into chest-voice vocalization and head-voice humming.

The other MacDiarmid cycle, *The Infernal City* (1971), commissioned by Duncan Robertson for Glasgow University's McEwen Concerts, forms the stony urban contrast to the previous cycle's rural paradise. It centres on poems about Glasgow and Edinburgh (it could be any big city: Berlioz's loathing for Paris and Wagner's for Berlin are musically evoked in the first song, which combines Berlioz's version of the *Dies Irae* with Fafner's theme from

The Ring); but Stevenson also introduces his Sorley MacLean setting, 'Calvary', in a new version for tenor and piano in the Scots translation by Douglas Young quoted earlier. Equally effective as it was in its choral garb, this song comes as a point of deep humanitarian repose after the frustration of the first MacDiarmid numbers, and the cycle brightens towards its conclusion with a passionate exhortation to 'Open Glasgow Up!' (dedicated to the memory of Charles Rennie Mackintosh), and a final vision of 'The Aerial City', Glasgow's immaterial antithesis glimpsed in paradisal cloud-shapes at dawn.

One might suppose that these years of intense concentration on Scottish poetry and music implied a narrowing of Stevenson's focus, away from the vast canvas of mingled national idioms adumbrated in the *Passacaglia*. But of course MacDiarmid had been a partial inspiration for that work, and to read MacDiarmid (as Stevenson did, constantly) was to engage with a mind humming with ideas and verbal echoes from all over the world. *In Memoriam James Joyce* remained an ever-present injunction to universalize his music by absorbing a myriad concrete particulars of national musical character.

Stevenson's growing interest in oriental music manifested itself during this rich song-writing period through some beautiful songs to words by the Indian poet-sage Rabindranath Tagore, and through two song-cycles with harp: *Vietnamese Miniatures* (1966), to poems of Ho Chi Minh; and *Nine Haiku* (1971), to Japanese poems of the school of Basho, in translations by Keith Bosley — a particularly exquisite example of Stevenson's musical inventiveness within a strictly limited formal compass. His idiom here blends Scottish pentatony with the chromatically inflected Japanese variety — a process which, pushed to an appropriate extreme in a modern haiku lamenting the atom-bomb on Hiroshima, issues in an agonizedly 'contemporary' 12-note total chromaticism. But these were still sketches of a larger concept. Remembering the Bantu drummer at Nyanga, Stevenson continued to ponder what a 'World Music' could be.

> I had heard in South Africa a development of rhythm that was far in advance of its use anywhere else. In comparison with the African rhythms I had heard, it was *we* who were the really 'tribal' people — the 'savages'. The Africans are the real sophisticates of

rhythm, and we possess no such cultivated rhythmic sense.

Then the experience of listening to Raga-playing made me realize that the sophisticates of melody are the Asians, and that we have no comparable melodic sense. Indian Raga-performers can sing twenty-two notes to the octave and finish up on the same note every time; whereas the greatest singers in the Western world often experience difficulty in singing twelve notes to the octave — the twelve semitones — in tune. When I asked myself what the European contribution to music has been, I saw very clearly that it is in harmony and counterpoint.

Then I began to wonder what would happen if I played a recording of an African drummer and superimposed on it the Indian Raga-playing without the Indian drums. What relationship would emerge from the association of these two things, if any? Problems like this came to my mind for the first time after going to South Africa, and then I realised that I had been feeling my way towards this new aesthetic rather than Busoni's — towards an idea of finding coalescent points in the music of different peoples.[6]

Stevenson was not the first composer to think this way (no-one can be first, it seems, with any creative thought). Certainly, Percy Grainger had a pre-vision of it in his *Scotch Strathspey and Reel* (whose piano version is one of Stevenson's favourite recital pieces). Grainger's programme-note to that joyous stramash (which is partly based on the Strathspey 'The Marquis of Huntly' by the great Scots fiddle-composer William Marshall, 1748-1833) imagines a jolly kind of 'World Music':

If a room-full of Scottish and Irish fiddlers and pipers and any nationality of English-speaking, shanty-singing deep-sea sailors could be spirited together and suddenly, miraculously endowed with the gift of polyphonic improvisation enjoyed, for instance, by South-Sea Island Polynesians, what a strange, merry, friendly Babel of tune, harmony and rhythm might result!

Grainger's mention of 'pipers' among his 'friendly Babel' is especially significant. Stevenson had provided the *Passacaglia* with a pibroch more or less by instinct, and at the last minute. But in further researches into the bagpipe and the *Ceol Mor* he began to grasp the

6. Composer's Anthology, p.751.

position Scotland might occupy in 'World Music' as a point of vantage, or indeed as a nexus of intermingling cultures. The harmonic implications of the Great Highland Bagpipe's traditional tuning (a nine-note scale from G to A, with the fourth and seventh degrees approximately a quarter-tone sharp, providing the only instance of microtonal music indigenous to the British Isles) were thought-provoking indeed:

> The scale contains five elements: quartatonic structure (found in Scotland's most ancient vocal music, the waulking songs); pentatonic modes (found in much African, American negro, Asian, Balkan, Czech, Hungarian, Polynesian and Scottish music); hexatonic modes (found in Scottish folksongs); heptatonic modes (found in ancient Greece and Rome and in most European music); and microtonal elements (found in Asian music, particularly Indian). It is thus the only scale to contain an amalgam of the world's scales. . . .
> The implications of the scale of the Great Highland Bagpipe embrace triadic and quartal harmony, major/minor harmony, and suggestions of microtonal harmony (. . . which are capable of realization in string writing). It is thus the only scale to contain an amalgam of the world's harmony.[7]

The ideas of 'world music' were expounded in Stevenson's book entitled *Western Music: an Introduction* (Kahn & Averill, 1971) — an elegantly-written and thought-provoking primer for students and general readers that views music in its social and human context, and traces it from its most ancient origins to the mid-20th-century pluralism of electronic music, jazz, pop, and the folk revival. The final chapter catalogues suggestive modern examples of Western composers employing aspects of Eastern music techniques, and *vice versa*, and speculates upon the emergence of a 'musical multilingualism' reflecting the world-experience of the human race:

> African music is primarily rhythmic and physical; Asian is primarily melodic and spiritual; and European music is primarily

---

7. Extracts from Ronald Stevenson, 'A Note on the Harmonic Implications of the Scale of the Great Highland Bagpipe', unpublished typescript dated 19 August 1971.

harmonic and polyphonic, emotional and intellectual. The sum
of the physical, the spiritual, the emotional and intellectual, is the
whole being of an individual's life. So the sum of world music is
the complete music of mankind. (*Western Music*, p.208)

A commission from the BBC for a piano concerto to be premièred
at the 1972 Henry Wood Promenade Concerts provided Stevenson
with an opportunity to explore this conception on a large canvas, and
in a much more systematic way than in the *Passacaglia*. The first
performance of his Piano Concerto No. 2, *The Continents*, in which
Stevenson himself was the soloist, revealed an extrovert work so full of
life, colour and variety that the listener is hardly aware of the firm
architectural structure that binds it all together. Essentially its thirty-
five-minute single movement (arranged in five 'continental' sections,
enclosed within a prologue and epilogue) is articulated as a series of
variations on a double theme: two old obsessions, DSCH (Example 3)
and 'Clavis Astartis Magica' (Example 2), turn out to be the mirror
image of each other, and are expressed now in contrapuntal
combination (Example 7).

Example 7

The Concerto's imaginative point of departure was a delayed
reaction to Stevenson's South African experience, crystallized in a
poem by the Afrikaans poetess Ingrid Jonker, prophesying that the
child-victim of the Sharpeville massacre will become 'a giant without
a pass-book', overriding all barriers, trekking through the world. *The
Continents* is a trek through the world's diverse musics. Each section
concentrates on one musical element and brings one orchestral
department into prominence. After the Prologue adumbrating the
concerto's thematic basis, the 'African' section is essentially a study in

complex rhythms, the piano being employed as a drum, and pitted against unpitched percussion. The second section (Australasia and Asia) consists of unharmonized or droned pentatonic melody, mainly on the strings, with the piano-strings plucked to give a pizzicato effect. Gradually the writing grows more polyphonic, as if approaching the counterpoint of Europe. Stevenson supplies a 'geographical' link, from an Indian raga played on plucked piano-strings, to the only European music with close affinities to the music of Asia: Scottish *Ceol Mor*, symbolized by a proud and stately quotation of Stevenson's own *Chorale-Pibroch for Sorley MacLean*.[8]

Europe, East and West, is then represented in the third section by two fugues for woodwind and piano. The first (marked *Andante dialettico*) is on a new theme created from the elements of DSCH and 'Clavis Astartis'; the second takes the form of an exhilarating dance in Bulgarian rhythm, accompanied by the soloist with a toccata-like *perpetuum mobile*. A fiery, brass-dominated Russian March (a recasting and elaboration of the 'Peace, Bread and the Land' variations from the *Passacaglia*) leads to the North and South American sections, which begin with a superbly smoky piano blues, wittily accompanied by a lugubrious viola, its part inflected by smoochy quarter-tones. Further delights include a hot-blooded Latin-American waltz and a cheeky piano rag uproariously taken over by the full orchestra, leading to a final section in which previously-heard fragments of the world's musics 'confront' each other, a hubbub of many voices against which the throbbing chords and flashing arpeggios of the solo piano sound out as the voice of a single human consciousness. No all-embracing solution is possible in this confrontation: polarities and problems remain. But the double theme (Example 7) returns calmly, diatonically broadened in the orchestra like a benedictory chorale, and the piano's chords toll like responses before the final thunderous agreement on an *Eroica*-like E flat.

---

8. Unbeknown to Stevenson, this effect had been foreshadowed fifty years before by the Manchester-born composer John Foulds (1880-1939), whose unpublished Concerto for wordless solo voice and orchestra, *Lyra Celtica*, had begun with a vocal cadenza in the Hindu 22-note scale before moving into

Example 8

Celtic pentatonic writing. Long before Stevenson, Foulds advocated a new musical language arising from the combination of Western and Oriental (principally Indian) musical techniques, and had taken some steps in that direction in his music. Stevenson did not become aware of Foulds's output (much of it remains unpublished) until the mid-1970s, but he has since been an enthusiastic champion of it, and has premièred several of Foulds's chamber and piano works.

Initial B from the Iona Psalter, c. 1200.

6

KNOTWORK (VARIATIONS)

Barred music — accented music — finds its ultimate form in symphony. Unbarred music — quantity music — expresses itself in pattern-repetition; hence the idea that the Celt has no architectonic power, that his art is confined to niggling involutions and intricacies — yet the ultimate form here is not symphony, it is epic.

Hugh MacDiarmid
The Islands of Scotland

STEVENSON has written no Symphony. *Ben Dorain* was at first announced as one; but when, or if, it finally emerges it will be without that designation, which would disguise its essential variation-form. The ethico-aesthetic strand in Stevenson's pacifism extends, rather startlingly, even to an avoidance of sonata-form, of musical structures which are rooted in *conflict*, whether of contrasted themes or keys.[1] His works, to be sure, are full of contrast and of bracing, pungent dissonance. But his favoured forms and textures are unitary, growing from a single subject — canon, fugue, passacaglia, variations — or from a single poetic or physical impulse: song, dance.

Symphony and other sonata-based structures apart, he has contributed to almost every major (and minor) musical form, and for an extraordinary variety of vocal and instrumental forces; though works for solo piano, solo songs, and choral pieces form the bulk of his *œuvre*. Indeed, he must count by now as one of the most prolific

---

1. There are, however, two mature works called Sonata — the four-movement Harpsichord Sonata (1968), which contains elements of the dance suite and whose fugally competing first-movement themes are held within bounds by a formal *ritornello* in the double-dotted manner of a Baroque French overture; and the Duo Sonata for harp and piano (1971), in a very unclassical two-movement form, whose first movement recapitulates its two themes simultaneously, refusing to give primacy to either of them.

composers of our century, rapidly approaching the unquantifiable work-totals of such comparably inventive figures as Heitor Villa-Lobos and Darius Milhaud (neither of whom pursued a parallel career as an instrumental virtuoso, as Stevenson has done).[2] Composers so prodigiously fertile seem, of their nature, less concerned with the perfection of each individual work than with the on-going creative activity that comes as naturally to them as breathing. Though Stevenson's works are always finely polished in their technique, and often long and deeply considered, he would be the first to admit that not everything in his output is of equal significance. In fact, one of its distinguishing characteristics is the extraordinarily heterogeneous array of pieces great and small, light and serious, profound and unabashedly trivial that jostle within it, like the obstreperous succession of incidents that make up any human life.

What are we to make of an *œuvre* which includes, at one extreme, the *Passacaglia on DSCH* – massive in scale, world-embracing in intention, of fantastic architectonic complexity – and yet, at the other, abounds in little album-leaves: such as the *Scots-Swedish Twi-Tune* of 1979, a mere 16 bars of Graingeresque *jeu d'esprit* that entwines the tune of 'The Bonnie Bonnie Banks o' Loch Lomond' and the Swedish folktune 'Ack Värmeland, du sköna', with intriguing harmonic consequences for them both? Any composer might occasionally let fall such a chip from his work-bench (even Schoenberg sometimes wrote little canons for his friends), but Stevenson's *œuvre* is so knee-deep with them, that one must conclude such companionable miniatures are as necessary to his creative life as are the much more ambitious compositions which he undertakes.

I choose the epithet 'companionable' with care. The manuscript of

---

2. There is no opera, but two have been projected at different periods. In the 1950s he sketched a one-act opera about the painter J.M.W. Turner; in the 1970s he mapped out a large-scale one loosely based on the Nazi show-trial of George Dimitrov, the Bulgarian communist leader falsely accused of complicity in the burning of the Reichstag. The still-extant wire recordings of the trial, with Dimitrov's courageous defiance of Hermann Goering, are a sound-document that moves Stevenson deeply, and coloured his conceptions of the vocal idiom of the proposed opera.

the *Twi-Tune* (exquisitely calligraphed, as are all his finished copies of his music), bears a dedication to 'my very dear friends Harry, Anna, Oscar and Leonora'. It requires some background knowledge to recognize that these names constitute a family; Harry Winstanley (a connoisseur of Gershwin and Godowsky), his Swedish wife (thus the combination of Scots and Swedish melodies), and their children; and an end-note that the piece was first 'thought out' in 31 Gayfield Square, Edinburgh, refers to the Winstanleys' home at the time. This is an act of music-making that is also a gesture of friendship.[3]

Friendship, homage, salutation — human contact at all levels, whether private and relaxed as in the *Twi-tune*, or public and rhetorically intense as in the vast Shostakovich-tribute of the *Passacaglia* — seems in fact one of the principal motive forces that drive Stevenson's music; perhaps the most important of all. His astonishing range of enthusiasms and acquaintance is faithfully mirrored in the dedications of his compositions, their titles, and the actual musical ideas with which he chooses to work. The various Busoni- and Grainger-inspired pieces are the most obvious examples, but one might instance such tokens of admiration as a *Threepenny Sonatina* on tunes from Kurt Weill's *Dreigroschenoper*, the *Doubles on Rubbra's Cradle Hymn* for organ or harpsichord (a Christmas offering to the English composer), or a 'contrapuntal re-working' of Duke Ellington's jazz classic *Mood Indigo*. Such works are metaphorically a hand clasped in friendship, sometimes over the centuries. Indeed Stevenson's entire concept of 'World Music' is perhaps the artistic equivalent of a gigantic bear-hug, attempting to sweep *everything* up in a single idealistic embrace of shared humanity. But many pieces can

---

3. The *Scots-Swedish Twi-Tune* has at least one successor, also dedicated to the Winstanleys: 'Ack Värmeland' is this time combined with a well-known Italian popular song to produce *Santa Lucia and the Star-Boys*, a little polyphonic study for piano referring to a Swedish winter festival of the light (for which 'Santa Lucia' has become a traditional tune) when the daughter of the house, crowned with candles, serves morning coffee to her parents accompanied by two 'star-boys'. Stevenson composed it in a train from Aberdeen to Edinburgh in 1982; the manuscript includes a tiny drawing of the train, looking more like a child's toy.

also be seen as fingers pointing, drawing attention to individual achievements and excellences we neglect at our peril.

A typical example is a little work composed in 1976, to which Stevenson gave the title *¡Ojala el nombre Casals resonase en las calles!* (Would to God that the name of Casals resounded in the streets!). A musical homage to the Spanish-born cellist Pau Casals — whose incomparable musicianship, simple humanity and determined rejection of the Fascist tyranny in his country all naturally excited Stevenson's admiration — it is cast in the rhythm of a sardana, the street-dance of Casals's native Catalonia, and is actually scored for *cobla*, the traditional Catalan wind-band. (There is also, needless to say, a version for solo piano.) The principal tune follows the intonation of the title, and the name 'Casals' — a great aspiring leap of a seventh — is echoed exultantly in various registers, as if shouted from street-corners and carried over the roof-tops.

Then there is the 'other' tribute to Shostakovich. In 1975 Stevenson was one of 13 composers from Europe and America (the only other Briton was Alan Bush) commissioned to contribute a short piano piece to a Soviet symposium being prepared for publication on Shostakovich's seventieth Birthday. In the event, Shostakovich did not live to see it, and the volume — *Dmitri Shostakovich. Stati i Materiali* (Moscow, 1976) — appeared instead as a memorial to him. All the composers made use of Shostakovich's 'DSCH' monogram in their compositions: even now Stevenson had not exhausted that figure's potential, and produced on this occasion a work completely unrelated to his *Passacaglia* — the *Recitative and Air*, a bare, brooding and profoundly (indeed prophetically) elegiac meditation, spun entirely out of permutations of the monogram at various transpositions, and closely akin to the attenuated textures and raw melodic eloquence of Shostakovich's own late works (Example 9). Despite its small size, the *Recitative and Air* is a highly characteristic specimen of Stevenson's genius for evoking character and fellow-feeling by purely musical means, and has a compelling magnetism that has drawn him back to it on several occasions, to make alternative versions for violin and piano, cello and piano, string quartet, and full string orchestra.

Practically all Stevenson's songs may be considered homages to the poets from whom he draws their words: he is an inveterate reader of poetry in many languages and dialects, as reflected in the totality of his vocal output. Many signal examples are considered elsewhere in this book. Here I would only touch on the sheer range of literary inspiration, from poems in Lancashire dialect (as in the choral cycle *Weyvers o' Blegburn*) to poems of ancient China and Japan; from classic figures of British literature such as Browning, Byron, or Tennyson to contemporaries such as Alan Bold, Kathleen Raine, and Sacheverell Sitwell. Two poets whom he has set many times and with particular fondness are James Joyce and that courageous invalid Scots lyricist, William Soutar. The composer's partial namesake R.L. Stevenson provided the texts for a paean to the beauties of the Border country in the song-cycle *Hills of Home* (1976); and a less-often-remembered Scot, John Davidson (1857-1909), is the poet of *Songs of Quest* (1974), a cycle for tenor and piano commissioned by the Schubert Society of Vienna. This cycle culminates in one of Stevenson's most thrilling and compulsively memorable songs, 'The Last Journey'. Here a fierce tramping or walking music, distantly recalling the idiom of Vaughan

Example 9

Williams's *Songs of Travel*, is translated into a cosmic, metaphysical image of human life, the poet seeing 'the Earth a-spinning on its nave' and heroically ever journeying 'round the world and back again'.

The largest of all Stevenson's instrumental 'homages', apart from the *Passacaglia*, is his Violin Concerto, commissioned by Yehudi Menuhin in 1977, finished in 1979, and dedicated to the memory of Menuhin's teacher, the wonderful Rumanian composer, violinist, Bach-interpreter and all-round musical genius, George Enescu (1881-1955). This is one of his most important works, yet has so far remained unplayed although the full score is complete down to the last detail. The Violin Concerto is a logical extension of the 'World Music' ideals embodied in Piano Concerto No. 2 as is made clear in another passage of the essay by James Reid-Baxter, which I quoted in connexion with the unperformed *Ben Dorain*:

> Beginning with a pentatonic dawn rāgā (which enables [Stevenson] to unify all the disparate folk elements utilised in the course of this 55-minute work), the first movement's opening 'song' grows into a dance as the violin is brought from India by the gypsies to Rumania. . . . [It] continues its journey through space and time in a homage to the Hardanger fiddle celebrated by Grieg in his *Slåtter*, a Norwegian wedding march becomes a Norse funeral march, and the finale begins with a 'strath-reel-jig' in which Stevenson combines the rhythms of all three Scottish-Irish fiddle-dances. It crosses the Atlantic in a square dance, and the cycle of day ends with night and the *Dies Irae*: dawn and dusk, East and West, song and dance, life and death are all shown to be ornamentations on the great circle of being.

Many other 'works of homage' could have been cited in this context. Stevenson's Nocturne for clarinet and piano, *Homage to John Field*, evokes without pastiche the style of the Irish composer who invented the Nocturne before Chopin, and helped found the Russian Nationalist school of composers. *Ostinato Macabre on the Name Leopold Godowsky* invokes the great Polish composer-virtuoso whose transcriptions of Chopin and whose musical impressions of Javanese *gamelan* music have equally excited Stevenson's admiration. Three Improvisations for descant recorder on themes by Emmanuel Moór remind us of the Hungarian composer, pianist and inventor of a double-keyboard piano. A *Birthday Prelude* for piano celebrates the

East German composer (and authority on British chamber-music) Ernst Hermann Meyer. A *Choral and Fugue in Reverse* combines a theme of Robert Schumann with one by his wife Clara. A *Kleines Triptychon* commemorates the Polish composer Czeslaw Marek, a pupil of Busoni who was in his nineties when Stevenson encountered him in Switzerland, and whose *Triptychon* for piano Stevenson considers a masterpiece. *Ragmaster*, one of Stevenson's many jazz-style pieces, is a homage to Eubie Blake. Variations on 'Sally in Our Alley' is, obviously, a musical compliment to the art of Gracie Fields. And so on, seemingly without end. The items just mentioned are merely a random selection from Stevenson's catalogue of works — a catalogue, moreover, multiplied by innumerable transcriptions, employing every conceivable level of re-working of their originals, from composers as diverse as Purcell, Ysaÿe, Van Dieren, Nielsen, Balfe, the blind 18th-century Irish harp-virtuoso Carolan, and the fiddle, pipe, harp and song composers of Stevenson's ancestral Scotland.

Such a catalogue can hardly be characterized as the achievement of a single man. Rather, Stevenson's output is in a curious sense the meeting-place, sometimes the hostelry, where the differences and diversities of much that is most treasurable in our musical traditions can be reconciled — but also celebrated: and where they may enjoy, in the old Scots phrase, 'a guid crack'.

Many of the pieces I have mentioned here are actually, or comparatively, miniatures: indeed it might be argued that Stevenson is a very rare case of a miniaturist of genius who completely transcends the limitations which that label usually implies. In a previous chapter I observed the paradox that the *Passacaglia* is ultimately founded upon a multitude of miniatures. What is it in Stevenson's art that so perfectly connects the epigram to the epic?

The answer, I am convinced, is variation. Variation, in all its forms from the decorative to the truly metamorphic, backed by a massive faith in Busoni's creed: the One-ness of Music. Stevenson is possibly the foremost living practitioner of all the techniques of variation,[4] as

---

4. One unusual example is the *Variations and Theme* for cello and piano (1974) in which, as the title implies, the basis of the structure only emerges at the very end, as the folksong 'The Bonnie Earl o' Moray'.

he is almost certainly the most dedicated exponent who has ever lived of that particular variational art we call transcription, or arrangement (notwithstanding his great exemplars, Busoni, Liszt, and even Bach!).

Transcription, the art of arranging a pre-existing work for another medium, flourished from the late 16th century (think, since Stevenson often does, of Peter Phillips's virtuoso arrangement for virginals of Caccini's madrigal *Amarilli*), and reached its climax in the 19th century with such prodigies as Liszt's piano arrangements of the Beethoven symphonies. It is a great tradition that has fallen on hard times in an age of musical purism, where scholarship strives to establish the *Urtext*, the precise particulars of what the composer originally wrote, as the sole authoritative form of any given work. Such prescriptive academicism is one of Stevenson's bugbears: but he and it are really concerned with different issues. Scholarship very rightly tries to establish historical facts, or at least the limits within which the facts may be located. The transcriber is interested in the continuing potential of musical ideas, whether for wholesale re-shaping or for transference into a new medium. On this topic (as on so much else) Busoni went to the root of the matter when he made the fundamental observation that the act of composition is *itself* an act of transcription: the composer's ideas precede his notation of them, that notation being simply one possible form the ideas could take. 'From this first transcription to the second is a comparatively short and unimportant step', he wrote; and also

> from [Bach] I learnt to recognize the truth that Good and Great Universal Music remains the same through whatever medium it is sounded. But also the second truth, that different mediums each have a different language (their own).

Even if confined to a straight arrangement of music so that it can be played in another medium, the aesthetic decisions involved in transcription are such that it constitutes a species of variation. It is not merely a question of re-distributing the notes, but of finding the registers, the chord-spacings, the necessary dynamic and harmonic reinforcements by which those notes will sound idiomatically and effectively on the new instrument. Here a doctrinaire adherence to the text will inevitably result in a weakening of the musical *Idea*; in the hands of a master-transcriber, like Liszt, Busoni, or Stevenson, the music's macro-structure may remain more or less intact, but its microstructure may undergo extensive recomposition.

Stevenson has a particular relish for the compositional challenges posed by transcription, and for realizing the latent potential of musical riches all too often locked away in the lumber-rooms of our musical culture. From portions of Berg's *Wozzeck* to W.C. Handy's *St Louis Blues*, he has brought all his love and skill to bear on the task, and in the course of his labours has produced 'artistic collaborations' that deserve to rank with the greatest in the field.

The six unaccompanied Violin Sonatas of the Belgian violinist-composer Eugène Ysaÿe (1858-1931), written in 1924 for six violin-virtuoso friends, are known to most violinists — if only by reputation — as a rarified peak of their instrument's repertoire, a latter-day counterpart of the solo sonatas and partitas of J. S. Bach. In an amazingly short time, from November 1981 to January 1982, Stevenson recomposed all six of them as piano sonatas, doing much of the work in trains between concert engagements. Since the sonatas total seventeen movements in all, this was tantamount to composing the Bach-Busoni Chaconne in D minor seventeen times over! Stevenson's re-thinking of the music for two hands, his creative extension of Ysaÿe's already rich harmonies, the thought (and notation) required to bring melodies through decoration on the new instrument, and a myriad other details testify to his consummate mastery of the art of transcription. At the end of the second movement of the First Sonata — a two-voice fugue to which Stevenson has contrived to add a completely integral third part — he wrote, with justifiable pride: 'This is the proof of what I have learned from Bach, Busoni and Godowsky'. Yet this is no isolated feat — comparable ones include the Grainger *Hill-Song No. 1* mentioned in a previous chapter; solo piano versions of the first-movement *Adagio* from Mahler's Tenth Symphony and of Carl Nielsen's titanic organ work *Commotio*, and the transformation of Van Dieren's Fifth String Quartet into a piano sonata.

Like many a transcriber before him, Stevenson sometimes in-corporates transcriptions — even self-transcriptions — into original works, or uses them as the point of departure for new structures. We see this in his *Peter Grimes Fantasy* on themes from the opera by Benjamin Britten: another instance of Stevenson's reviving the old tradition of 'operatic fantasy' as he had already done in the *Faust* triptych (and later in a piano suite drawn from Paderewski's little-known opera, *Manru*). Commissioned by the BBC for a television première in 1972, the *Grimes Fantasy* is a terse yet stunning exercise in transcendental virtuosity. No pot-pourri, it takes Britten's themes and develops them into an entirely new form, dramatic in its own (pianistic) terms. Structurally, the work is an inspired fusion of fugue with aspects of sonata, conveying the essential melodic and episodic information about the opera's character-conflict through the rise of the music associated with the mob, and the fall of that associated with Grimes; this is interwoven with the famous 'Storm' interlude, and the cold 'Dawn' music appears last, as a cold, shocked coda of plangent, silver-grey sonorities.

This magnificent fantasy was an earnest of Stevenson's friendship with, and regard for, Britten, developed over several visits to the Aldeburgh Festival. That esteem is further commemorated in a transcription for chamber orchestra of one of the *Walztes* Britten wrote (and mis-spelt) as a young boy; and by the *Sonatina Serenissima* (1973-77), a gently elegiac piano work whose four brief movements refer obliquely to Britten's final opera, *Death in Venice.*

To embrace Busoni's vision of the One-ness of Music is to realize that there is no such thing as originality in art, only perpetual rediscovery and endless interconnexion of ideas on which the artist puts his individual stamp. Stevenson's output is an immense lived testimony to this simple truth. He might also claim that it is a particularly Celtic truth, and quote in support the provocative opinion of an Irish composer who successfully combined folk and 'classical' traditions, Sean Ò Riada:[5]

---

5. Quoted from Ò Riada's posthumous book *Our Musical Heritage*, edited by Thomas Kinsella (The Dolmen Press, n.d.). There is of course a Stevensonian 'homage', the piano-work *A Rosary of Variations on Sean O'Riada's 'Irish Folk Mass'*, composed in 1980.

Every day the sun rises, every day it sets. Every day possesses the same basic characteristics, follows the same fundamental pattern, while at the same time each day differs from the last in its ornamentation of events. The particular events of each day are, to the basic pattern of days, as the particular ornamentation of each verse of a song. This is the idea that has lain at the root of all Irish traditional art since pre-Christian times. It is represented in the carved stones of the great burial-ground at Newgrange, in the curvilinear designs of the Book of Kells, in the old mythological stories, episodic and cyclic in form, in all Gaelic poetry — even in James Joyce's *Ulysses* and *Finnegans Wake*; and in the *sean-nós* singing which still survives as an art form today. The basic pattern of the song remains in each verse, but the events, the ornaments, vary. This does not necessarily mean that the musician who does not use variation is a bad one; he is a passive holder of tradition. The musician who makes good variations is, on the other hand, a creative contributor to the tradition. He makes it grow and develop.

7

THISTLES AND ROSES

So here I hail all the fellow-artists I know
And all the singers and narrators everywhere,
'A rum lot they are, as the Devil said when he looked
over the ten Commandments.'

Hugh MacDiarmid
So here I hail all the fellow-artists I know

TO seek to express world culture, to coalesce separate traditions in a vast unity-in-diversity, is a truly heroic aim for a writer or a musician, yet one that inevitably invites the charge of *folie de grandeur*. Stevenson, like Hugh MacDiarmid, greatly admires Ezra Pound's *Cantos*, that monumental life-work — the 'poem including history'. Stevenson's music also includes history, a polyphony of elements chiming from earlier composers named and nameless. Pound intended to provide a 'universal poetry', synthesized from luminous examples of the world's culture, history, language (and music), and his pages are therefore peopled with the names and voices of artists, doers, and speakers, who exemplified for him true quality in human civilization. Yet since Pound's grand synthesis took place inside one very idiosyncratic mind, the *Cantos* are, as poetry, so eccentrically individualized, even solipsistic, as to be accessible only to the small number of readers willing to make the required intellectual effort. This of course was partly his intention: the ideal reader is directed towards the texts Pound studied, and encouraged to become as curiously learned as the author. But many would further argue that Pound's personal foibles, his anti-semitism and support for the Fascist regime in wartime, disqualified him from serious consideration as a poet, and inevitably disfigured his art, whatever the beauty or vigour of individual lines.

That was not the opinion of MacDiarmid, Pound's antipodes in politics: he admired Pound all his life, and the *Cantos* are a clear influence on *In Memoriam James Joyce*. Yet even some of MacDiarmid's

English poems are hardly readable without recourse to a dictionary, and in his quest for synthesis he packs them densely with the fruits of his reading in science, aesthetics, philosophy, and the world's literatures. He too is, deliberately, 'hard work' for his readers; and some find the brandished thistle of *his* politics — the combative conjunction of Marxism and Scottish Nationalism, sometimes proclaimed with superb scorn and pungency, sometimes rantingly obsessive — altogether too prickly to grasp. His 'Vision of World Language' can, like Pound's, seem compact of particulars so *recherché* that the vision remains obstinately private.

Stevenson, in discussing MacDiarmid, puts this in proportion:

> MacDiarmid, for all his perhaps unequalled array of stupefying allusion, is by nature decidedly not a scholar, no erudite. He seizes upon any and every fragment of fact and fantasy, bundles it into his ragbag until it is full — and then empties it in a niagaran spate of poetry. He is an apocalyptic ragman among contemporary poets.[1]

Stevenson himself is by nature more scholarly; but a prime characteristic of his *œuvre*, if we attempt to view it as a whole, is *its* 'stupefying range of allusion', and he too is something of an 'apocalyptic ragman' of music. His favoured method of discourse in articles and lectures is pre-eminently allusive, allowing one topic or figure to suggest another, and weaving a grand synthesis through the web of words. Sometimes, as in 'MacDiarmid, Joyce, and Busoni', the synthesis is profound, the illumination immense. Elsewhere the formula 'this reminds me of …' or 'and here I think of …' pulls in some fleeting resemblance (verbal, musical, or philosophic) to the topic in hand, drawn from another denizen of Stevenson's well-stocked personal pantheon — maybe leaving the reader or listener wondering how deep, how actual, the similarity was, and what if anything it demonstrated. These digressions seem less like hard argument than symbolic gestures of artistic comradeship, a brief salute asserting a commonality of minds and hearts. Such symbols are vitally important to Stevenson; his music is full of them.

---

1. MJB, p.152.

In one sense the very nature of music gives him an advantage in communication over MacDiarmid or Pound. Few Westerners read Chinese, but many more can hear the beauty in a Chinese pentatonic tune. Stevenson's music is not politically polemical in the way MacDiarmid's poetry is. He often quotes Busoni's apothegm that, in seeking to illustrate the phrase 'a poor but contented man', music can represent the contentedness but not the poverty, which is 'a phase of terrestrial and social conditions not to be found in the eternal harmony'. But that does not mean that politics is forgotten, nor the effect he thinks his music should have in the real world; and he has never made any secret of his political sympathies — far to the left, doubly rooted in his working-class origins and his sense of Scotland's nationhood.

> To communicate in a real and direct sense — the sense of speech — that is for me the greatest challenge at the present time. If one looks at the unemployment figures in Britain... and relates them to the map, one can see very clearly that unemployment is far more prevalent in the north than in the south. Thus the kind of music that can express the feeling of the north is a very different kind to that which evokes the mood of the south. For the northern music will be tough-textured and born of struggle.... I feel it as a personal challenge to try to write music like this — for the very reason that this kind of expression has been realized so little. The music I write in this way may be worse professionally — inferior to the music written by some southern composers. *It may be crude. I hope it is, for I think it needs to be.*[2]

This attitude informs much of Stevenson's work, though the resulting 'crudities' have less often been in the texture of the music (which is almost always very finely wrought) than the emotional reactions which it, or his presentation of it, may arouse in certain sections of his audience. A typical case was the response which his Sorley MacLean settings for chorus, *Anns an Airde, as an Doimhne* (described on p.63), drew from the committee of the Greenock Gaelic Choir.

A faction of the committee disapproved of the text of 'Calbharaigh'. One of them protested: 'Mr. Stevenson, we know

---

2. Composer's Anthology, p.752 (my italics).

there are slums: we don't want to sing about them'. While not wishing to underestimate the often sterling work achieved for the cause of Gaelic by An Comunn Gaidhealach, I do believe this response to MacLean's 'Calbharaigh' typifies an all-too prevalent attitude fostered by the choral repertoire sung at the National Mod.[3]

It is of course ironic that when it came to be sung, this particular song (both in its choral and later solo versions) was widely recognized as one of the most sheerly and calmly beautiful of Stevenson's vocal works.

Precisely because the poem was so shot through with pain, that was the very reason why I considered the music to it as very still and contained, to allow the words to speak. If the image is not too pious or flowery, all I wanted to do was enhalo the poem in melody.[4]

For many critics those words must seem paradoxical. Presumably most contemporary composers approaching 'Calbharaigh' would attempt a dissonant, 'Expressionistic' setting, believing they were thereby doing justice to the social discords the poem reveals, rather than according, as Stevenson does, prime importance to melodic beauty and verbal clarity. There will be musicians for whom his image is indeed all too 'flowery' — and who would object to the use of the word 'flowery' itself (as in the bedridden Scots poet William Soutar's dying glorification of nature in *The Flowery Lea*, a poem Stevenson has taken for the title-song of a Soutar song-cycle) as altogether too prettified and *passé* for the grim realities of the 20th century.

Or rather, not *passé*: plain old-fashioned and sentimental. When Stevenson is quoted, as he was very recently, inveighing against the state of comtemporary pianism —

There is no grace in the style of playing, no elegance, no charm. Pianists no longer 'sing' with their fingers. . . . I feel much the same about a great deal of the music that's being written today. . . . There's a lack of grace, a lack of poetry, a lack of beauty.[5]

---

3. MacLean, p.178.

4. MacLean, p.178.

5. *Scotland on Sunday*, 26 February 1989.

— there must be some who wonder what kind of 'modern composer' Stevenson thinks he is. Is he not too unreconstructed a Romantic even to be considered 'Post-Modern'? Many of his heroes, his symbolic comrades-in-art, are not even names to ordinary concert-goers and musicians, while to most musicologists they are names only, in encyclopedias, above small (and usually inaccurate) paragraphs. Surely 'World Music' and the compositional development of Scots folk music are impossibly quixotic causes, alike irrelevant to a musical culture whose cutting edges are to be found (depending on your favoured brand of modernism) in computer and electronic composition, the various forms of 'Minimalism', or in the transformational wizardry of post-post-Webernian serialism? Are they not even more irrelevant considering how tiny that brave new world of musical culture is, compared to the vast majority of the population which makes no distinction between Stevenson or Stockhausen (except that the latter is a better publicist), since both of them are 'classical' rather than 'pop' musicians, and therefore for switching off?

These are unfairly rhetorical questions, compacted from things I have heard said by others, and from questions one must occasionally entertain for oneself, if one's critical standards are not to degenerate into complacent axioms; all of them must long ago have been pondered by a man as thoughtful as Stevenson. But the idea that there is some special quality that constitutes a modern composer is a delusion. *Everything* (pop and jazz included) written today is modern music; much of it is dross and some of it is flecked with gold. Time alone (and then only if assisted by the questing intellects and sympathies of future generations) will sift out the nuggets of true value. All questions of style and medium are essentially matters of fashion. Bach himself was considered a hopeless old reactionary by his clever composer-sons.

Stevenson sometimes quotes approvingly a dictum of Nikolai Medtner (another 'hopeless reactionary' who was in fact a peerless piano composer): 'What is modernism? The fashion for fashion... the tacit accord of a whole generation to expel the Muse ... and instal Fashion in her place as the autocratic ruler and supreme judge'. These

Ronald Stevenson.

are grand words — we are all against mere Fashion, are we not? — but talk of 'whole generations' is dangerously sweeping. Modernism is surely rather a form of Puritanism: exclusive, prescriptive, concerned to identify true faiths and true paths forward, severely limiting their number. Its first commandment is Originality, rather than character. It forgets (did Medtner also forget?) that true creativity is founded on appetite, on the artist's willingness to follow his own inclinations: to multiply within the world examples of the things he loves. This Stevenson is certainly doing, and it makes him not so much a Romantic as a 'Sciomantic', in the sense in which he once wrote about his friend Sacheverell Sitwell (some of whose poems he has set as songs): 'Both Busoni and Sitwell are masters of sciomancy, the art of divining the future from the shades of the dead'. Beyond Lethe, the shade of Anton Webern is weightless as that of Emmanuel Moór.

Stevenson expends much less of his energy in polemic than, say, MacDiarmid did; but he never shrinks from a good argument, and has sometimes given hostages to the 'modernism' debate by impatient or intemperate remarks on contemporary musical trends. On occasion, he seems by implication to dismiss much that others (not necessarily less thoughtful than he) may consider moving and enriching musical experiences.[6] But I suspect the doubts expressed about him on 'modernist' grounds are a smokescreen for the more basic reactions that Stevenson arouses: that he offends against the modernist version of good taste. For in espousing 'old-fashioned' values in art and life, and readily confronting primal human emotions with traditional forms that entirely by-pass modernism's ways of keeping them at arm's length (by indirection, formalization, distortion or satire), he exposes his human vulnerability, and dares us to expose our own.

In many ways he really is a very 19th-century figure, with the (sometimes rather alarming) larger-than-life quality, a natural theatricality or staginess, that reflects a more heroic age. He disconcerts by his taste for the grand humanitarian gesture, his

---

6. Stravinsky, over the years, has been a particular bugbear; though I believe Stevenson is less concerned to question his worth as a composer than the value of making him the admired model from whose basis so much late-20th-century music starts.

eagerness to associate his music with the mind-numbingly large issues of our time — as when he dedicates the pedal-point variations of the *Passacaglia* 'To Emergent Africa', and its third fugue 'In memoriam the Six Million Jews', or alludes, in the more recent *Motus Perpetuus(?) Temporibus Fatalibus*, to the threat of nuclear extinction. In a less committed composer such dedications would seem pretentious posturing, but the music tells us he is utterly sincere. Still, some people seem to find such gestures very 'un-British' (correction: un-English). They do not complain when Shostakovich dedicates a string quartet 'In Memory of the Victims of Fascism and War'.

Not only does Stevenson stand as a mephistofaustian composer-pianist in the pattern of Liszt, Busoni and Paderewski (who of the three he physically most resembles), but he also fits the mould of such great Victorian artist-socialists as John Ruskin, or the Transcendentalists Emerson and Thoreau, for whom art and life and nature were all compact. When Stevenson includes pages of Ruskin's prose — on the surpassing excellence of mountains — in the solo horn part of his *Bergstimmung*, and enjoins the player to read them before performance, he is attempting to inculcate an attitude of mindfulness, of the spiritual realities for which his musical notation, however precise, is at best only a symbol. Stevenson warmly shares Ruskin's admiration for the pre-Raphaelite painters, especially Rossetti and Burne-Jones. Long 'out of fashion', and stigmatized as 'escapist', their works are nowadays creeping back into critical estimation: not only because of their beauty and superb technique (always admitted, as if that was of no consequence), but because they dealt in an archetypal symbolism that retains power and meaning from century to century.

Above all he has the 19th-century capacity for spontaneous emotion, and is unafraid to show it. Poetry, of which he remains a voracious reader, often and openly moves him to tears — a reaction much more common in Victorian times than in our frigidly fastidious century. Tears nowadays tend to provoke embarrassment, to be looked down upon as a confession of weakness, or sentimentality.

Probably no work of Stevenson's is more tailor-made to provoke this kind of *de haut en bas* criticism than the very large collection of piano transcriptions he wrote at intervals between 1980 and 1986 and collectively entitled *L'Art nouveau du chant appliqué au piano* (with the significant subtitle 'Studies in the lost art of *Bel Canto* pianism'). This is a direct reference to the Austrian pianist Sigismond Thalberg (1812–71), remembered as one of the greatest virtuosos of the 19th century but, except to pianophiles, entirely forgotten as a composer: and in particular to his *L'Art du chant appliqué au piano* op.70, a set of arrangements of operatic arias used as teaching pieces for piano. (Thalberg was one of the few composers who closely studied singing, and was especially admired for the 'vocal' quality of his piano tone.) Stevenson's work, like Thalberg's, consists of twenty-two transcriptions — chiefly of Victorian and Edwardian popular songs, some of them treated very simply, others with enormous bravura and complexity. Also significant is Stevenson's general dedication: 'To the memory of my beloved father'. With *L'Art nouveau du chant* he has in a sense returned to his roots, to the parlour in Blackburn, to that childhood fusion of piano tone and tenor voice as the cardinal symbol of music that reaches the heart. Some of the songs now transcribed in this collection were, in fact, among his father's favourites.

And so here, transformed into 'singing piano pieces' with enormous artistry and simple love, are such 'old chestnuts' as F. Nicholls Crouch's *Kathleen Mavourneen*, Stephen Foster's *Beautiful Dreamer* and *Jeannie with the Light Brown Hair*, Coleridge-Taylor's *Elëanore*, Vincent Wallace's *In Happy Moments Day by Day*, Maud Valérie White's *So we'll go no more a-roving* (which Percy Grainger called 'one of the greatest songs of all time'), Sigmund Romberg's *Sweethearts* (treated as a waltz in canon-form), and many more, including an Irish Folksong (as arranged by Hamilton Harty), a Neapolitan one (as sung by Caruso), and songs by Frank Bridge, Rachmaninoff, F.G. Scott and Reynaldo Hahn. Cynicism is wholly out of place here. One wonders if there is another composer living who would be able to adorn, en-halo, en-flower this particular repertoire as Stevenson has done, wholly without satirical intent, even apparently without irony.

Perhaps irony is occasionally there: the version of *La Mattinata*, for instance, faithfully transmits Leoncavallo's pedalling as heard in his 1904 phonographic recording of the song with Caruso, includes a silvery filigree cadenza marked 'con delicatezza paderewskiana', and climaxes in a 'perorazione alla Jussi Björling', with a downward white-key glissando imitating an Italian tenor's vocal 'swoop' and a final gigantic keyboard-spanning 32-note arpeggio in homage to (but huger than) the chords in the Paganini-transcription from the fourth book of Busoni's *An die Jugend*. But the irony is entirely affectionate: all this delightful elaboration is accomplished for the sheer joy of it, and nowhere does it detract from the projection of the melody. Clearly, *L'Art nouveau du chant* represents one of Stevenson's supreme efforts as a transcriber, fully comparable with his versions of the Ysaÿe sonatas. Yet critics who might think the latter an acceptable (if slightly maverick) activity for a composer to engage in may balk completely at the former. It is the very *unblushingness* of Stevenson's delight in unwrapping these melodic sweetmeats of yesteryear that undermines our own attempts at sophistication.

A related emotional reaction may be provoked by a song-cycle written towards the middle of his labours on *L'Art nouveau du chant*: the *Lieder ohne Buchstaben* (Unspelt Songs) of 1982, to texts by the Australian poet A. D. Hope. These are ardent love-songs, in a clearly 20th-century idiom, yet with a romantic sumptuousness of accompaniment: but the music adorns frankly erotic verse whose sensuality is treated with an equally frank sensuousness of melody and harmony, rising to peaks of lyric fervour that would grace any 19th-century aria that implied the same things with circumspect periphrasis. In another composer we might expect satire (perhaps at least a blues); here we blush because none is intended.

In my experience, reactions to Stevenson's music tend to be strongly for or against; he is a controversial figure, and clearly to some people a disturbing one. I think what disturbs some critics is that his ethical and aesthetic attitudes imply there can be a direct transference of the emotions, sympathies or ideals which we experience in art into those of our daily lives — whereas many people seem to want art to be something entirely *apart* from their daily lives, a separate and self-contained ritual. The artist's faith that something will indeed carry over perhaps implies a fairly simple conception of the workings of the imagination. But the risks in this coalescence of the artistic imagination with the everyday are surely less impoverishing or distorting than any theorizing which would keep them asunder. There is no simple Art/Life antithesis. Rather, art must relate to all other activities which, *together* with art, are the necessary components of our lives. In its gestures, its attitudes, and its feelings, Stevenson's music does this constantly.

8

DON QUIXOTE IN ALBA

> ... it must be thought of as a craft
> In which the consummation of the idea, not in analysis
>   but in synthesis,
> Must be the subject of the object — life.
>
>   Hugh MacDiarmid
>   *Lament for the Great Music*

STEVENSON once wrote:

> I think all great art aspires beyond nationalism, as an exploration of occult regions of experience. But I am convinced that a people's culture cannot get beyond nationalism until it has *realised* it. Scotland hasn't.[1]

If we are to get his music, and its 'nationalism', into perspective, that is surely a cardinal statement. It is also ultimately a statement of metaphysical belief, incapable of objective proof. In what might the 'realization' of Scotland in music consist, and to what level must it be realized? How many elements will have to be brought in, how many composers will have to use them, before it can be deemed to have taken place? Yet, in a general sense, Stevenson is almost certainly right. Can anyone seriously believe that contemporary Hungarians like Ligeti and Kúrtag (whatever one may think of their music), could write as they do had not Bartók and Kódaly thoroughly tilled the soil of Hungarian folksong, and thereby created a national style? Scotland's folk-music is at least as rich as Hungary's, and Stevenson has striven to bring it, and its possibilities, into the general consciousness, out of the kailyard and beyond the scholarly confines of ethnomusicological treatises. He has not been alone in this, but he seems to have had the most all-embracing view, and to have made the most comprehensive use of it — in conjunction with European and

---

1. Letter dated 30 April 1968 to the musicologist Ates Orga; quoted by him in his article 'The Piano Music of Ronald Stevenson', *Musical Opinion*, March 1969, p.292.

other 'classical' traditions — in his own works.

Since the Violin Concerto was completed in 1979 we have heard less from Stevenson on the subject of 'World Music' (the ideal has not been put aside, but is being worked at in smaller and separate acts of synthesis). But Scotland, her music, and her political destiny have increasingly become central creative issues. He has been a tireless proselytiser and educator, delivering long impromptu radio-talks on his poet-friends MacDiarmid, Goodsir Smith, and Sorley MacLean in Australia in 1982, and preparing and presenting for Radio Scotland three marathon series of programmes: six on Pibroch and the MacCrimmons of Skye (1980), ten on the music of the Celtic Harp (1982), and six on the fiddle music of North-East Scotland, *Maisters o' the Bow* (1984). He arranged much of the music for the latter two series; and though based on meticulous research they were in no sense academic, but sought to interest a broad spectrum of listeners in the riches and diversity of these folk-traditions.

The past decade has been a period of unusual richness in his own compositions. Quite apart from the transcriptions, songs, and piano pieces mentioned in the last two chapters, Stevenson has moved away from direct quotation of Scottish folk-sources to a personal enlargement and extension of their characteristic idioms — most radically in the sphere of chamber music. Paradoxically, one of the means by which he has brought this about is through intensified concentration on the possibilities of that arch-construct of 20th-century modernism, Arnold Schoenberg's 12-note technique.

It is possible to exaggerate this tendency, of course. In fact, Stevenson has always deeply respected Schoenberg's idealism, and took account of the Viennese master's 'method of composition with 12 tones related to one another' even in the chamber works of his late teens. One of his earliest and loveliest piano transcriptions was of Marie's Lullaby from Alban Berg's *Wozzeck* (1953 — dedicated to Luigi Dallapiccola); and many subsequent works make some use of 12-note themes or tonal schemes, generally treated in an unsystematic way for harmonic colouring or chromatic intensification. He has spoken to me of Schoenberg's method as 'a Jacob's Ladder to the stars', possibly *contra natura* but not, as some arch-conservatives might hold, a betrayal of the principles of Western Music — rather, a supreme act of musical idealism.

His preference has generally been for note-rows whose construction naturally yielded triadic formulations, reasserting the validity of tonality from a new perspective. A tiny example is that archetypal Stevenson song *The Skeleton of the Future* (composed in Capetown in 1964), where the tenor's wide-leaping, declamatory setting of MacDiarmid's poem is poised upon a note-series divisible into the four triadic forms — major, minor, augmented, diminished — symbolizing the four colours mentioned in the text, with the polarity of black and white represented by the black-key gloom of E flat minor and the white-key radiance of C major.[2]

A looser example may be found in the rapt, enchanting *Wasserfall bei Nacht I* (1981), one of the most delightful of Stevenson's numerous songs to words by the gentle German poet and mystic Christian Morgenstern. Here the piano's peacefully descending opening figure, a 12-note series of three triads linked by three chromatic passing-notes, repeated from high register to low, reflects the ceaseless motion of the falling water; and though the ensuing song is in no way serial, its themes and figures draw continually upon this initial formula.

A deeper philosophical involvement with the expressive potential of 12-note methods, however, seems to arrive in the very remarkable Duo for Spanish guitars, *Don Quixote and Sancho Panza*, which Stevenson composed in 1982-83: a twenty-five-minute epic that surely counts among the most important guitar compositions of the last twenty years. Cast as a sequence of 'Goya-esque bagatelles' (in the Beethovenian sense, and viewing the *Diabelli Variations* itself as a bagatelle-sequence), this Duo is a set of amazingly graphic programmatic variations, enacting the salient events of Cervantes's novel from the interpretation (suggested by a remark of Hugh MacDiarmid's) that the Knight of the Sorrowful Countenance and his peasant squire are archetypes of the two possible human philosophies,

---

2. The 'triadic 12-note' technique here is very close to that independently evolved by Stevenson's friend Bernard Stevens, who indeed towards the end of his life composed a piano Nocturne on the note-row from this Stevenson song.

Ronald and Marjorie Stevenson.

the Idealist and the Materialist. The guitarists therefore assume these opposing roles. Don Quixote's music is serial, based upon a 12-note row of ascending and decending fourths — an abstraction, beautiful and painful, from the artificial conditions of equal temperament. Sancho Panza has only the seven notes that make up the three primary triads, and is earthily at ease in his tonality. Their dialogues and ensembles provide some of Stevenson's most ingenious, humorous, and eventually deeply moving music of recent years. The episodes include dances, serenades, a fugue ('Don Quixote thinks and sighs: Sancho Panza dances and laughs'), homages to Barríos, to Pedrell (a stern mediaeval chant of the Passion of Christ from his *Cancionero*, adorned by scarifying on-string glissandi), and to Fernando Sor (whose special notation of harmonics, perhaps never since employed,

Stevenson adopts for the most achingly beautiful variation, Don Quixote's Address to the Goatherds concerning the Age of Gold). There is also a full-scale depiction of 'Master Peter's Puppet-Show', complete with fanfares and Moorish battle, and a puppet-minuet tune that, once lodged in the memory, refuses to leave it. To its strains, the foolishly wise Don Quixote realizes he has been nothing but an 'Übermarionette', a puppet of larger forces (the concept is Edward Gordon Craig's), and Sancho leads him home to die. The tragic finality of the ending has a dark, truly Spanish *duende*.

Save that it is a Scottish composer's personal commentary upon a much-translated treasure of world literature, there is nothing specifically Scottish about *Don Quixote and Sancho Panza*. But it was soon followed by a self-proclaimedly *Scots Suite* for unaccompanied violin (1984) that is scarcely less remarkable a conception. The title is perhaps deceptively modest: this is a six-movement *tour-de-force* patterned after the solo suites of Bach, yet its refined distillation of the Scots folk-fiddle vernacular into an idiom of uncompromising density of texture and rhythmic freedom makes it a worthy successor to the solo Sonata of Bartók. The movements include a 'Pibroch-Fugue' which assimilates the characteristic ornamentation of bagpipe variation to violinistic polyphony (Example 10); a magisterial Strathspey; and a gloriously inebriate Jig which the composer, on the occasion of the first complete performance (in 1988, by Leonard Friedman) whimsically christened 'The Drunk Man looks at the Fiddle'. He did not bother to point out that the jig is also a serial invention, with a 12-note theme that appears in inversion and retrograde in approved Schoenbergian style.

A perhaps more symbolic marriage of Stevenson's tonal-serial concerns with Scottish ones is a work for horn and piano of 1986: *Bergstimmung*. The title-page translates the German as Mountain Mood, but also gives the Scots Gaelic equivalent, *Bean-Fhonn* — and, by a typically Joycean pun, the piece is at once an evocation of nature, of mountains, and a memorial to Alban Berg on the fiftieth anniversary of the Austrian master's death. Here Stevenson creates tonal (and 12-tonal) variations out of permutations of the 4-note figure BEDG (=BER[e]G), the horn literally conjuring echoes from

Example 10

the ambient air as the player directs the bell of his instrument onto the reverberant strings of the piano.

But the most dazzling recent coalescence of Scots and European themes undoubtedly takes place in the extraordinary Fantasy Quartet for piano, violin, viola and cello (1984–85), to which Stevenson gave a macaronic Latin-Gaelic title: *Alma Alba* — the soul of Scotland.[3] It is a single movement lasting about fifteen minutes, packed, bursting at the seams, with riotous invention. No actual folktunes are used, though folk idioms are continually referred to, absorbed into and extended through Stevenson's personal language. After a vigorous introduction, the opening section evokes the music of the Celtic harp, of Pibroch (the *Chorale-Pibroch for Sorley MacLean* takes another bow;

---

3. 'Alba', the Gaelic name of Scotland, is itself a word echoing ancient history, demonstrating Gaelic's distant descent from Sanskrit in its correct pronunciation 'Al-a-pa', with the residual Sanskrit *svarabhakti* vowel that is inserted between two consecutive consonants.

this time the strings correctly inflect it with bagpipe-scale quarter-tones), and the Scots fiddle. The central slow section is an eloquent *Andante*, full of dramatic colour, in the style of a Border Ballad, with a broad and lyrical theme that just happens to be a 12-note idea. There follows a Fugue on a different but related 12-note theme that develops into some of the most intensely chromatic writing Stevenson has ever produced; and finally an astonishing Quodlibet. In his Violin Concerto Stevenson combined the rhythms of Strathspey, Reel and Jig in the solo violin part: here, violin, viola and cello play these three dances simultaneously in riotous polyphony (more like what the veteran Soviet composer Miaskovsky was wont to call 'muchyphony'!), companionably swapping themes while the piano keeps up a grotesque commentary.

This garrulous, impassioned, obstreperous work disconcerted some listeners when it was first broadcast, and indeed on a single hearing it may sound like a loose succession of brilliant episodes,[4] ending in a stramash of Bax and Bartók thrown together with the anarchic gusto of the American pioneer Charles Ives (the Quodlibet is the nearest thing to his *Hallowe'en* Scherzo for piano quintet I have ever heard). But further hearings, and a study of the score, have convinced me of the work's superb organic unity, which Stevenson secures by means of his perennial mastery of variation and by a very special brand of serial working. The entire materials of the work derive from the piano's three opening 4-note chords, encompassing all 12 notes of the chromatic scale. The chordal presentation, however, allows the order of pitches in the 4-note segments to remain unfixed, and Stevenson fashions his themes from different orderings within the segments, a method that resembles Schoenberg less than it does

---

4. In fact many Stevenson works have given this initial impression (Piano Concerto No. 2 certainly did so), only corrected by better acquaintance; the general comprehensibility of Stevenson's idioms tends to conceal the fact that his music takes just as much 'getting used to' as do the creations of any complex mind. Since he habitually thinks in terms of variation, its immediate foreground tends to be occupied by strongly-contrasted episodes; the deeper background unity needs time to emerge.

the 'troping' techniques of Schoenberg's Austrian contemporary, Josef Matthias Hauer. Hauer's own music, however, is almost devoid of rhythmic and polyphonic interest: Stevenson's is afire with both. Two possible orderings of the chords would reveal continuous chains of perfect fourths or fifths, the intervals to which the open strings of violin, viola and cello are tuned — and thus just as the main 12-note melodies in *Alma Alba* are related, so are they intimately related to the folk and fiddle tunes in which the work abounds.

The style of the Fantasy Quartet has since been extended in *The Gangrel Fiddler* (1987), a raw and tangy song-cycle in Aberdonian Doric to poems by Donald Gordon, set for baritone, piano and an eldritch obbligato violin part requiring a very fine player for its proper interpretation. Meanwhile Stevenson has pursued other serial-motivic obsessions, notably in the dauntingly virtuosic piano toccata written in 1987-88 for the American pianist Joseph Banowetz and called *Motus Perpetuus(?) Temporibus Fatalibus* — 'Perpetual(?) Motion in Fateful Times'. The query is integral to the title: Stevenson associates it with the ever-present threat of nuclear catastrophe. In its hectic, driven 'perpetual motion' and incessant motivic metamorphosis, the music suggests a frenzied feat of creativity on the very verge of extinction. It is as if the enormous generative power of *Passacaglia on DSCH* has been concentrated into a confined space (ten minutes duration) at immensely high pressure. The result is an unremitting showpiece of cumulative rhythmic tension, founded on a 12-note series that combines the sigils of BACH, DSCH, FB (for Busoni), and (for Schoenberg) ASCH. It relates closely to the *Dies Irae* chant, which is drawn into the proceedings as the toccata — which has the character of a hectic night-ride — develops into a pulverizing *Totentanz.*

As Stevenson has used all these cyphers separately in previous works (and three of them in combination in the *Passacaglia*: see Example 5), this stunning perpetuum mobile might be viewed as a serially-organized kaleidoscope of all the pregnant chromatic symbols that have so obsessed him over the years and so deeply interfused his harmonic language. The restless, intricate permutations of the note-row and the motifs derived therefrom hark back to the 'Cavalcata notturna' movement of the *20th-Century Music Diary*; and by a fine paradox they allow Stevenson's continuing commitment to the Lisztian tradition of pianistic diablerie to emerge all the more clearly.[5] The piece does not so much end as vanish out of sight on the crest of an upward-rushing chromatic spiral, as if suggesting that its variation-processes continue elsewhere, unabated.

Motus Perpetuus(?) promises to be the first of a series of very fast toccata-like piano studies on which Stevenson finds himself embarked. Its immediate successor is *Dodecaphonic Bonfire*, which approaches the 12-note question from yet another angle. Written for a première within a Conference during the 1988 Edinburgh Festival to mark the tenth anniversary of Hugh MacDiarmid's death, it takes its cue from the lines in *In Memoriam James Joyce* glossing a famous comment of Schoenberg.

> Other masters may conceivably write
> Even yet in C major
> But we — take the perhaps 'primrose path'
> To the dodecaphonic bonfire.

Stevenson here combines the white-note C major scale with black-note pentatony to arrive at a 12-note vocabulary that simultaneously embraces both. The next in the series will be *Le Festin d'Alkan*, currently being completed; and the next the test piece commissioned for the 1990 Scottish International Piano Competition in Glasgow.

Not that Stevenson has become any kind of born-again serialist. In the deepest essence of his musical being he is an incorrigible eclectic.

---

5. As man and artist, Liszt remains a prime inspiration for Stevenson — symbolized most recently in an expansive and very beautiful solo piano work to mark the centenary of Liszt's death, the *Symphonic Elegy for Liszt* (1986). Commissioned by Stevenson's friend Peter Hick, a doctor of medicine who is a 'pianophile extraordinaire' and who has also commissioned the forthcoming *Le Festin d'Alkan*, the *Elegy* — ably premièred in London in 1989 by the pianist Brian Davidson — presents an inspired osmosis of Liszt's and Stevenson's characteristic idioms, with almost no direct quotation from the Hungarian master but a kaleidoscopic evocation of the forms with which he is most associated, notably Barcarolle, Perpetuum mobile, and a kind of 'Scoto-Hungarian Rhapsody'.

As he remarked in a radio programme on the traditions of the Irish harp, 'Every age has its purists and eclectics; they seldom understand each other, but surely a catholic view of culture admits both'. His eclecticism is founded in his deep belief in Busoni's twin principles of *Junge Klassizität* and the One-ness of Music, and the human value he places on companionship. Several recent scores illustrate this in quite different ways.

The song-cycle *A Political Panel* (1985-87) is the fulfillment of an unrealized design of Busoni's. On the outbreak of the 1914-18 War, Busoni conceived the idea of a song-cycle in the languages of the four principal combatants (German, French, Italian, and English) as an artistic gesture against the divisions created by nationalist hysteria, but did not carry it beyond some sketches for a song to a poem by Carducci (the others were to be by Poe, Hugo, and Heine). In the spirit of this concept Stevenson has made settings in the same four languages, but of different texts. The first is of the last poem, 'Memories and Premonitions', which Busoni wrote on his death-bed in 1925; then comes Cocteau's 'Noël à la fin de la guerre', a poem addressed to his mother on Armistice Day, and D'Annunzio's apostrophe to the greatest European poet of the Middle Ages, 'A Dante'. The cycle ends with Byron's 'By Babylon's Waters'. The music here is a version of Busoni's own youthful setting of that poem, while the other songs are each developed from passages in other works of Busoni — respectively from the Second Violin Sonata, the *Sonatina in Diem Nativitatem*, and from *Faust*. Thus, yet again, transcription merges into a new musical conception.

A major song-cycle on R.L. Stevenson's *A Child's Garden of Verses*, commissioned by the BBC to mark the centenary of the publication of that classic of poetry for children, and setting no less than seventeen of the poems for tenor or young soprano (with optional boy treble) and piano, reaffirms Stevenson's commitment to the pristine vision of childhood. He conceived it not as an 'Album for the Young' but as 'Scenes from Childhood', lavish in its compositional and pianistic bravura, partly seen and sung from the child's viewpoint and partly recollected in adult tranquillity. The long and richly allusive final 'Envoy' is as moving an expression of the mature man's debt to childhood experience as Stevenson has ever composed. Its antithesis is to be found in *The Harlot's House* (1988), an eerie dance-poem (it would make a superb ballet) directly inspired by the verses of the poem by Oscar Wilde, scored with astonishing resourcefulness for the unlikely combination of free-bass accordion and a huge array of percussion. Victoriana and 20th-century Angst here meet in surely the strangest of all Stevenson's sets of variations on the *Dies Irae*, with a Strauss Waltz, a Quadrille, a Rag, a Dance of Death, and a welter of freshly-imagined techniques to render the poem's many musical allusions: at one point the accordion imitates horn tone, while bowed vibraphone impersonates a violin.

Two recent choral works perhaps best sum up the sheer range of Stevenson's invention. The four *Peace Motets* (1984–87) for SATB choir are innocent of all quotation or stylization: short, almost epigrammatic settings of single Biblical phrases or sentences in a spare, unadorned tonal style whose straightforward harmony and discreetly canonic textures are designed to give maximum prominence to the ethical burden of such injunctions as 'Thou Shalt Not Kill' and 'Put up again thy sword into his place'. The poised, pellucid homophony of the final number, a setting of the Seventh Beatitude ('Blessed are the Peacemakers'), lingers long and fragrantly in the memory (Example 11, p.109).

Wholly different is the motet for 12-part triple chorus, *In Memoriam Robert Carver*. Stevenson has been increasingly drawn to the Carver Masses and Motets preserved in the so-called Scone Antiphonary, virtually the only surviving relics of the brilliant achievements of Scots sacred polyphony, otherwise deliberately obliterated by the Reformation. The latter-day rediscovery of these works in actual performance, after long neglect, has established Carver as a towering figure in Renaissance music, and an eloquent symbol of Scotland's suppression of the cultural glories vital to her sense of nationhood. Stevenson's interest was doubtless whetted by his friend James Reid-Baxter, a founder-member of the Carver Choir of Aberdeen, dedicated to the resuscitation of this repertoire. At Christmas 1985, the experience of singing the cantus firmus in a performance of Carver's four-part Mass, *Pater Creator Omnium*, inspired from Reid-

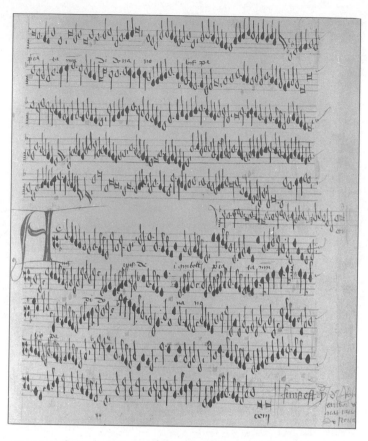

Opening of Mass by Robert Carver, from the Carver Choir Book, c. 1520.

Baxter's pen a poem in honour of Carver, written in 16th-century 'aureate' Scots, the literary language of Carver's contemporaries Dunbar, Henryson and Gavin Douglas. In 1987-88 Stevenson took Reid-Baxter's poem as the basis for his motet, which also refers to the Carver Mass. From the opening 'sciomantic' invocation, with Carver's name repeated 'like calling-up the dead', *In Memoriam Robert Carver* deploys a vast gamut of sound, using the entire vocal spectrum from deepest bass to highest soprano registers, in techniques ranging from the florid decorated polyphony of Carver's own early music to massive, dissonantly contemporary chordal homophony, threaded upon the declamation of a single tenor who expounds the poem like a cantus firmus around which all the other inventions gather. There are chilly, onomatopoeic wind effects; and Stevenson allots the choruses several Latin phrases in addition to those already in the poem, so the two marmoreal languages, Latin and Scots, counterpoint each other as text and sub-text. Thus the Catholic formula *Pater Creator* flowers suddenly into an 'extended family' — *Mater Creatrix, Filius Creator, Filia Creatrix*, and a huge unison: *Omnis Vitae*. The crucial word *Pax* opens onto a visionary evocation of the 'Easter Vespers' music from Busoni's *Faust* (which intones the same word); a later near-quotation of a famous cadence from Allegri's *Miserere* seems justified less on motivic grounds (though they are there) than as another symbol of stratospheric aspiration, hinting at 'occult regions of experience'. The final bars build up a vibrant, rainbow-like 12-note harmony to match the poem's 'soondand colours o' Eternitie'.

EPILOGUE

I asked John McInnes of the School of Scottish Studies: 'Who is a Gael?'. I didn't say 'What is a Gael?' — like the question that was asked of Kódaly: 'Who is a good musician?'. That doesn't mean Schubert or Busoni or Duke Ellington. Kódaly said: 'He who has a well-trained ear, a well-trained hand, a well-trained mind, and a well-trained heart' (and he didn't mean jogging!). And to 'Who is a Gael?', John McInnes said: 'One who has the language'. That's a very important answer at the present time. If a Chinese can speak Gaelic, he is doing more for Gaeldom in its death-throes than somebody born in the Isle of Skye whose orthography makes a mockery of it. (Which it generally does, even in distinguished writers. I know Gaelic writers who don't even know the correct word for Peace, which is *Sith*, 'Shee' as in 'Banshee', from the Irish Gaelic. The Banshee is the woman of peace, she s not a weird ghost, she comes through this terrible barrier, in those last moments of life, to take one back whence one came: Mother Earth, the White Lady, the Lady of Peace.)

Now I'm only an amateur etymologist. But I have learned, and I imbibed very early on, the Scottish language of music, and that is all that matters to me. And I know now that I speak it in music, fluently, without thinking about it. So much so that I didn't know that the ending of the Carver Motet returned to its first four notes — A,B,D,E: the essential motif of Scottish music.

Ronald Stevenson in conversation
at West Linton, December 1988

*I*N *Memoriam Robert Carver* and the *Peace Motets* both received their premières in late 1988, in remarkable performances by the young Scottish choral group Cappella Nova, in two 'Concerts for Peace' celebrating Stevenson's sixtieth birthday, held in Old St Paul's Church, Edinburgh, and in Glasgow Cathedral. As he faces his next decade of unwearied creativity, Stevenson remains as ever a companionable family man, whose persistence in his chosen path would surely have failed without the grit, support and commonsense of his wife Marjorie and the satisfaction of bringing up their talented children. With his son a violin-maker, one daughter a well-known actress, and the other a fine harpist and composer in her own right, Stevenson would seem to have founded an artistic dynasty!

He is still an idealist with strong roots in reality. Still a committed pacifist, he has no illusions that world peace will arrive overnight, or maybe ever, or that the human race will suddenly deny its baser nature and revert to some Age of Gold. Nor does he believe that Scotland's nationhood will revive quickly, to some blueprint of perfection. But some people must have the courage to embody such principles in their individual lives; to show that an alternative exists. Life may be, as Hugh MacDiarmid once said to him, 'the stern reflectit i' the mire'; but in this apocalyptic age, Ronald Stevenson's life-work speaks volumes for the virtues of astronomy.

Example 11

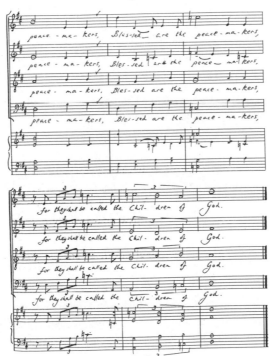

CHRONOLOGY

1928   Ronald Stevenson born on 6 March in Blackburn, Lancashire, younger son of George Stevenson, a railway fireman of Scottish descent, and Elizabeth Blundell, a mill-worker of Welsh descent.

1936   First piano lessons.

1943   First attempts at composition, songs etc.

1943–45 Accompanist and composer of music for Blackburn Ballet Company.

1945   Wins open scholarship to the Royal Northern College of Music, Manchester, where he studies (until 1948) piano with Lucy Pierce and Iso Elinson, composition with Richard Hall. Composes Sonatina No. 1 for piano.

1946   *18 Variations on a Bach Chorale.*

1947   *Hommage to Hindemith, War* for voice and piano, Violin Sonata, Sonatina no. 2; *Songs of Innocence* begun. First public piano recital (in Blackburn).

1948   Imprisoned as a conscientious objector to National Service, successively in Preston, Liverpool, Birmingham and Wormwood Scrubs. *Chorale Prelude for Jean Sibelius.*

1948–49 Working on the land at Freighting Hall, Essex, and later ditching and draining with Irish navvies. *Songs of Innocence* completed. Afterwards long out of work. *Three Nativity Pieces, Fugue on a Fragment of Chopin, Fantasy on Busoni's Doktor Faust.*

1950   Visits Gerda Busoni in Stockholm. *Fugue on Clavis Astartis Magica.* In Autumn becomes music teacher at Boldon Colliery School, Durham, where he remains until early 1952.

1951   Piano pieces and brass band arrangements. Orchestrates
        Van Dieren's *Weep you no more, Sad Fountains. Berceuse
        symphonique* for orchestra.

1952   Settles in Edinburgh. Marries his second cousin, Marjorie
        Spedding.

1952–63 Teaches in various Edinburgh schools.

1953   Birth of son Gordon.

1955   Six-month sojourn in Rome at the Conservatorio di Santa
        Cecilia, researching Busoni and studying orchestration
        with Guido Guerrini.

1956   Makes his home in West Linton, Peeblesshire. Birth of
        daughter Gerda. First meeting with Hugh MacDiarmid.

1958   Concert tour in the Western Isles.

1960   Begins *Passacaglia on DSCH* on Christmas Eve.

1961   Birth of daughter Savourna.

1962   On 18 May completes *Passacaglia on DSCH* in a
        preliminary version, presented to Dmitri Shostakovich
        during the Edinburgh Festival that year. Begins *Ben
        Dorain*.

1963   Visits East Berlin. Becomes Senior Lecturer in
        Composition, University of Cape Town. 10 December,
        premières *Passacaglia on DSCH* there, in its definitive
        version.

1964   Records the *Passacaglia* in a limited edition record set
        issued under the auspices of Cape Town University.

1965   Returns to Scotland and enters on a career as a freelance
        composer and pianist.

1966   Receives Arts Council Award under Scheme for Living
        Artists. Tours of Italy and East Germany, where he gives
        European première of *Passacaglia on DSCH* at Handel
        Festival, Halle. John Ogdon gives the UK première at
        Aldeburgh Festival.

1967   Harriet Cohen International Music Award. John Ogdon records *Passacaglia on DSCH* for EMI, and the work is published by Oxford University Press.

1968   Visits the USSR as guest speaker, 4th Congress of Soviet Composers, Moscow; and Bulgaria, where he performs the *Passacaglia* in Sofia.

1971   Premières song-cycle *Border Boyhood* with Peter Pears at the Aldeburgh Festival. Publication of book, *Western Music: an Introduction.*

1972   Premières song-cycle *The Infernal City* with Duncan Robertson at Purcell Room. Takes solo part in première of Piano Concerto No. 2 at Royal Albert Hall Promenade Concert. Tour of British Universities with the doyen Busoni student Edward Weiss, performing Busoni's *Fantasia contrappuntistica* (two-piano version).

1973   Lecture-recital at Aldeburgh Festival on the 'Transcendental Tradition' of piano transcription.

1974   Premières song-cycle *Songs of Quest* with Francis Loring in Vienna. Scripts, introduces, and performs in BBC2 television film on Busoni, 'Harlequin and Faust' (producer, Barrie Gavin).

1976   First of many Swiss concert tours, organized by Albert Wullschleger and Heinz Luscher. Recitals, concert and radio talks for CBC Vancouver, Canada. Recitals in the Liederkranz, New York, and for Ella Grainger's birthday in White Plains, New York State, USA.

1977   Music for BBC Scotland television documentary on Hugh MacDiarmid, 'Hammer and Thistle'.

1979   Completes Violin Concerto, commissioned by Yehudi Menuhin.

1980   Begins compiling *L'Art nouveau du chant appliqué au piano.* Concert tour of Australia. Grainger Memorial Lecture/ Recital at University of Melbourne. Broadcasts for ABC.

1981	Recitals in Switzerland to mark the 40th anniversary of Paderewski's death; gives a 'Faust' recital at the Goetheanum, Dornach.
1982	Completes piano transcriptions of all Ysaÿe's solo violin sonatas. Grainger Centenary recitals in Australia and at Aldeburgh Festival.
1984	Guitar duo, *Don Quixote and Sancho Panza. Scots Suite* for solo violin.
1985	Completes Fantasy Quartet *Alma Alba* and song-cycle *A Child's Garden of Verses.* In the winter of 1985-86 visits China, where he plays the *Passacaglia* in Shanghai, and then Australia, where *Bergstimmung* is composed.
1986	*Symphonic Elegy for Liszt.* Recordings of Grainger and Ronald Center issued by Altarus Records.
1987	Spring: takes seminars in piano literature at the Juilliard School, New York. Also performs *Passacaglia* there, after which the composer and former Busoni student Otto Luening makes a speech from the auditorium, acknowledging Stevenson as 'heir to Busoni'. Autumn: composer-pianist in residence, York University, conducting a course on 'The Political Piano 1789-1976'.
1988	Issue of Stevenson's own recordings, for Altarus records, of the *Passacaglia on DSCH* and operatic transcriptions, including the *Prelude, Fugue and Fantasy on Busoni's 'Faust'.* Many works performed at various 60th Birthday concerts, including premières of *Scots Suite, Faló dodecafonico,* and *In Memoriam Robert Carver. The Harlot's House* performed at the Edinburgh Festival.
1989	June: premières in Edinburgh of *St Mary's May Songs,* for soprano and string orchestra, and *Corroborree for Grainger* for piano and wind band. *Beltane Bonfire* composed as test-piece for 1990 Scottish International Piano Competition.

INDEX OF NAMES

INDEX OF WORKS

TRANSCRIPTIONS:

University of Houston Libraries